The Quest for Becket's Bones

The Quest for Becket's Bones

The mystery of the relics of
St Thomas Becket of Canterbury

John Butler

Yale University Press
New Haven and London   1995

Set in Palatino
Printed in Hong Kong through World Print Ltd

Library of Congress Cataloging-in-Publication Data

Butler, John R.
      The quest for Becket's bones / John Butler.
            p.   cm.
      Includes bibliographical references and index.
      ISBN 0-300-06115-3
      1. Thomas, à Becket, Saint. 1118?-1170—Tomb.   2. Christian saints—England—Canterbury.   3. Canterbury (England)—Church history.
4. Relics—England—Canterbury—History.   5. Canterbury Cathedral—History.   I. Title.
DA209.T4B88 1995
942.03'1'092—dc20   94-30026
                                                                                                          CIP

A catalogue record for this book is available from the British Library.

Frontispiece Canterbury Cathedral: view from the Trinity Chapel to the west end showing the site of St Thomas Becket's shrine between 1220 and 1538.

Contents

Photographic Acknowledgements   vi
Acknowledgements   vii
Prologue: Raiders in the Night   ix

1   In Life and in Death   1
2   The Skeleton in the Crypt   35
3   Believers, Agnostics and Sceptics   43
4   Debating the Bones   58
5   Archiepiscopal Intervention   78
6   The Grave Revisited   95
7   Burned or Buried?   109
8   Five Hypotheses   135
9   A Mystery   156

Notes   170
Index   176

Photographic Acknowledgements

hristopher Wilson: frontispiece; Jim Styles of the University of Kent at Canterbury, with the kind permission of the Dean and Chapter of Canterbury Cathedral: viii, 5, 8, 18, 21 (both), 22, 24, (both), 28, 34, 79, 113, 145, 146, 163; Copyright British Museum, Department of Medieval and Later Antiquities: xii, 93, 108; British Library, Department of Manuscripts, by kind permission of J. Paul Getty, Wormsley Library: 2, 3, 6 (both), 77; British Library, Department of Manuscripts: 7 (top: Cotton Claudius DII f.73, bottom and 164: Cotton Claudius BII f.341), 12 (Add. MSS 17012 f.21v), 16 (MS Roy. 2 B vii f.291), 30 (MS Cotton Tiberius E. VII f.278v), 33 (MS Roy. 2 B vii f.292r), 42 (MS Cotton Claudius BII f.214v), 47 (Add. Mss 54782 f.55v), 81 (MS Harl. 5102 f.32), 85 (Kings 9 f.38v), 87 (MS Cotton Claudius BII f.2v), 94 (MS Harl. 5102 f.17), 111 and 116 (MS Sloane 2596 f.15), 133 (Add. MSS 17012 f.51), 164; Trinity College Library, Cambridge: 10 (MS R. 17. 1 f.284v/285r); SCALA, Florence: 11; Royal Commission on the Historical Monuments of England: 15, 18: Dr Eamon Duffy: 19, 118; Copyright Cathedral Gifts, Canterbury: 26; Victoria and Albert Museum, London: 29; Cambridge University Library: 32 (MS D. d. 73 f.5); British Library, Department of Printed Books: 38, 39 (both), 41; Courtauld Institute of Art, London: 45, 61, 68, 91; The Pierpont Morgan Library, New York: 88 (M302 f.4v); National Portrait Gallery, London: 112; The Royal Collection © 1994 Her Majesty The Queen: 121; Angelo Hornak: 134; The Dean and Chapter of Canterbury: 137, 155; Bibliothèque Nationale: 140; Courtesy Professor Ursula Nilgen, photo Biblioteca Herziana, Rome: 158; Bayerisches Nationalmuseum, Munich: 168.

Acknowledgements

In writing this book I have received a great deal of help and encouragement from many people, and am most grateful for their various contributions. It would be invidious to rank them according to the magnitude or value of their help, so I simply list them in alphabetical order. I would, however, like to express my particular thanks to Richard Blaber for his valuable help in searching the Library and Archives of Canterbury Cathedral, and to Lou Opit for his stimulating and imaginative ideas. John Simpson, Dean of Canterbury, and Christopher Lewis, Dean of St Albans, kindly read and most helpfully commented on a draft of the book.

My thanks go also to John Baldock, Robert Baldock, Thomas Chough, David Earlam, Press Secretary of Canterbury Cathedral, Derek Ingram Hill, Canon of Canterbury, Sheila Hingley, Librarian of Canterbury Cathedral, Cherry Johnstone, Lois Lang-Sims, Sheila Lee, Rhona Lewis, David Macey, Receiver General of Canterbury, Graham Manley, Jackie Newton, Roger O'Brien, Jill Relton, Margaret Sparks, Michael Stansfield, Acting Archivist of Canterbury Cathedral, Jim Styles, Kate Urry, and Victor de Waal, formerly Dean of Canterbury. I am also very grateful to the many vergers and guides at Canterbury Cathedral, unknown to me by name, who have patiently and carefully answered my questions. None bears any responsibility for whatever shortcomings, inaccuracies or imperfections the book may contain.

ODET
DE COLIGNY
CARDINAL
DE CHATILLON
BISHOP
OF
BEAUVAIS
1517
1571

Prologue: Raiders in the Night

In the early hours of 14 August 1990 two young men, Peregrine Prescott and Risto Pronk, both of them former Foreign Legion adventurers, were arrested in the precincts of Canterbury Cathedral.[1] They had with them a map of the Cathedral and an array of housebreaking equipment – a crowbar, bolt croppers, a cold chisel, a club hammer, tin snips, a wire hoist, a reel of wire, masking tape and a torch. Three days later they pleaded guilty at the Canterbury Magistrates' Court of going equipped to burgle the Cathedral. Both men were given a twelve months' conditional discharge and their tools were forfeited. The true purpose of their mission has never been disclosed, but Prescott and Pronk told the magistrates that their intention had not been to steal anything of value but rather to prove that the tomb of the French Cardinal Châtillon (Odet de Coligny), in the Trinity Chapel of the Cathedral, contained the mortal remains not of the Cardinal but of the martyred Archbishop of Canterbury, St Thomas Becket.

The Trinity Chapel, which is one of the glories of Canterbury Cathedral, was completed at the end of the twelfth century. It forms the eastern end of the building, beyond the choir and the high altar, and it was designed specifically as the setting for the magnificent, bejewelled shrine that was to contain the relics of St Thomas. In a ceremony of great solemnity in 1220, almost fifty years after his death in 1170, Becket's remains were placed in the shrine, having been buried during the interim period in a modest tomb in the crypt. The shrine, which was the object of pilgrimage and veneration for generations of visitors to Canterbury, remained in the Trinity Chapel for more than three hundred years until the English Reformation. It was finally demolished by King Henry VIII's Commissioners in 1538 in a furious orgy of destruction of the tombs and relics of the English saints. The jewels and precious metals from the shrine were carted off to the King's coffers in London, and the mortal remains of Becket disappeared.

The plain and unadorned tomb of Cardinal Châtillon lies wedged at a curiously irregular angle between two pillars at the south-east end of the Trinity Chapel, very close to the location of St Thomas's shrine between 1220 and 1538. Together with his brother Gaspard, Odet de Coligny was

Canterbury Cathedral: the tomb of Odet de Coligny (Cardinal Châtillon) in the Trinity Chapel.

a leader of the Huguenots in sixteenth-century France, and he came to England in 1568, probably to enlist the help of Queen Elizabeth in the Huguenot cause. He died (or, some say, was murdered) in Canterbury in 1571, and his body was placed in a temporary coffin and lodged in the Cathedral pending its repatriation to his native France by his friends. That, however, never occurred, and the coffin, which was later encased in a protective shell of plaster and hessian, remains to this day in its odd position in the Trinity Chapel.

By way of explaining their actions, Peregrine Prescott and Risto Pronk told the Canterbury magistrates that they believed Coligny's death in 1571 had been faked in order to allow Becket's remains to lie in peace in the temporary coffin, next to the site of the erstwhile shrine. They claimed that Coligny's real burial place in France was known to the Church in that country, which, if true, might explain why the French authorities have never wished to have the coffin returned. It had been Prescott and Pronk's intention to force open the Cardinal's coffin and remove a piece of bone, an action which they evidently believed would resolve the issue. Their mission, however, was aborted by the vigilance of the Cathedral's staff, and Coligny's coffin remained undisturbed. Following the incident, a press release from the Cathedral offices commented that 'the Dean and Chapter can think of no reason why the tomb should be the target of these defendants unless they were acting on false information'.

At the time of the escapade Peregrine Prescott was living in Essex and Risto Pronk in Holland. According to a report in a local Essex newspaper, they had embarked upon the mission on behalf of Stanley Williams, whom Prescott had met in the Philippines. Williams, together with his father and an unnamed French professor of archaeology, wished to test the theory that the remains of Becket had survived the destruction of the shrine in 1538 and had somehow been secreted in Coligny's tomb. The exact part that Prescott and Pronk were to play in the enterprise was not clear; but they presented themselves as more than mere burglars. 'We think this is very serious', Prescott was quoted as saying, 'and we think people should know the bones are in there. We knew no one was going to believe us if we went to the Dean or the Bishop. They would just have laughed at us.'[2] The chairman of the Magistrates' Bench was moved to comment that 'this is the most remarkable explanation that we have ever heard in this court'.

Two weeks after the story appeared in the *Kentish Gazette*, the paper published a follow-up letter over the pseudonym of 'Thomas Chough'.[3] In the letter 'Chough' claimed that, although Prescott and Pronk's hypothesis was manifestly implausible, it was nevertheless true that the mortal remains of Becket had survived the destructive purposes of King Henry VIII's Commissioners in 1538 and been secretly reburied in another part of the Cathedral. According to 'Chough', the site is known to a handful of people in each generation who, in July and December each year, pray there for the conversion of England. He claimed that, among those who knew about this alleged coterie of silence, were a former treasurer of Canterbury Cathedral, Archdeacon Julian Bicker-steth, and a former Archivist of the Cathedral, Dr William Urry. Bickersteth died in 1962 and Urry in 1981.

The bizarre episode of Prescott, Pronk and Williams was merely one, if perhaps the most exotic, in a series of attempts to prove that the human remains of St Thomas of Canterbury still exist and can be located. The accepted wisdom on the matter is quite the reverse. The orthodox answer usually given by the Cathedral guides to those who enquire about the fate of Becket's bones is that, following the destruction of the shrine in 1538, they were taken out of the Cathedral, burned, and the ashes scattered to the winds. Some guides add the embellishment that the ashes were cast into the nearby River Stour or even fired from a cannon. If this was indeed their fate (and, as will be seen in Chapter 7, there is certainly strong evidence to support it), then that is the end of the matter: if the bones were consumed by fire in 1538, they cannot exist today. Yet the evidence in favour of burning, weighty and impressive though it is, has never, over the years, been sufficiently conclusive to put an end to alternative speculations about the fate of the saint's remains. Many of them are well known to those who visit the Cathedral and speak with the staff who work there.

Whose remains rest in the two unmarked graves in the north aisle of the eastern crypt? Who, if anyone, lies beneath the irregular and unidentified ledger slab near the altar of St Mary Magdalene in the north transept of the crypt – a slab that is embossed with the cross of Canterbury and is almost identical to the one covering the tomb of Archbishop Stephen Langton in St Michael's Chapel? Does the disturbed pavement immediately to the south of this slab, in the Chapel of St Nicholas, conceal a grave, and if so, whose? Why is the lamp that burns above the altar of St Mary Magdalene red, the colour of a martyr? Is there a grave behind the altar of Our Lady in the Undercroft, and if so, whose? And is there a parish church somewhere in east Kent that, as one popular legend has it, unknowingly harbours the bones of the saint, whither they were secretly conveyed and concealed by the monks of the priory in advance of the arrival of the King's Commissioners in 1538?

Of all the many speculations, none has aroused greater interest, or been as well founded, as that which sprang dramatically to life on 23

January 1888, when workmen excavating parts of the crypt of the Cathedral uncovered a hitherto unknown collection of bones. The finding sparked an intense debate about the fate of Becket's remains that continued for many years and that provides an intriguing story of mystery, politics, science, conjecture and romanticism. However, before turning to the bones and the curious circumstances in which they were found, the historical and locational context of the discovery must first be sketched.

Head of St Thomas Becket; 14th-century pilgrim's badge.

1   *In Life and in Death*

Thomas Becket, the thirty-eighth Archbishop of Canterbury, was born in Cheapside, in London, in about 1118.[1] His parents were Normans who had settled in the capital: his father was a successful merchant, and his mother was said to have dreamed that her son would one day be dedicated to God in a special way. Becket entered the service of Theobald, Archbishop of Canterbury, and quickly commended himself to his patron, who sent him to study canon law at Bologna and Auxerre before appointing him Archdeacon of Canterbury. Theobald was so impressed with his young protégé that he commended him to the future King Henry II, who in turn soon fell under Becket's spell. Shortly after his accession to the throne in 1154, Henry appointed him Royal Chancellor, and for seven years the two men were close friends as well as political allies. Though of a deeply religious nature, Becket, in the service of the King, was a considerable statesman and a daring and relentless soldier during the English campaigns in France. Tall and strong, he was often impetuous, violent and full of fury; yet he could also be courteous, inspirational, generous and diplomatic.

In 1162, with misgivings and premonition, Becket was consecrated Archbishop of Canterbury in succession to Theobald. From the outset he saw that his understanding of the duties of his office in defending the authority and jurisdiction of the Church would bring him into inevitable conflict with the King. He was to be proved tragically right. From the moment he resigned the chancellorship on the ground that it would be a worldly hindrance to higher work, Becket's antagonism towards his former friend and ally deepened. After some prevarication, he refused to consent to the Constitutions of Clarendon, which defined the extent of the King's customary jurisdiction over the ecclesiastical courts, and eventually he fled to exile in France in 1164.

A temporary restoration of the relationship was effected at Fretteville, in northern France, during a conference between the King, Becket and Louis VII of France in July 1170; but already another disputation had broken out between the two men. The King resolved that his son, Henry, should be crowned King during his own lifetime and, in Becket's absence in France, the coronation was performed by his ecclesiastical beatus eth Vignt

Ou cuncil escriez sen parr
Gent encuntre chescune parr
z demandent la beneicun
Ist chescun a sun cūpaignun
eer le leal aduocat
eu be sul pur li cumbat
Al neutrenomie rumeur
es par un cūmun parlement
suissent cūmun turt troi
arcuesq̇ il elu roi
ur parle lad e pur ueu
ensemble sunt turt troi uenu
Dune e dautre parr grant gerr
z pur la pes isunt present
z roil henric uint uolentiers
ar dui li curent messagiers
e larcuuesq̇ seint desi
e merriort pur en sa mei
uant turt surent assemble
li roi li cunte e li lettre
arcuuesq̇ sen humilie

sper le roi henri se plie
li dist beu sire roi
rendez sil uus plest a moi
a cause titre a uus cumand
aurez enz uostre cumand
restiure a uostre plaisur
l abandun a grant laisir
auf lonur de deu f
ue li roi henris sem
lus est urez be nest leim
quam blesse se seint diagun
dub hai tam mal assis
es bienr b par moi est mis
uisseir turner au roi de france
e dird oez grant dereuance
um ore muet desceod enseine
ar Wenelar e par sofisme
bi turt ruuer sul le descend
tur faru entrendre kauur
ar par cest mot sauf lonur
e deu nus mer turt en errur

Detail of the coronation of the young Henry III (from the *Becket Leaves*).

Left: Negotiations in France break down: Becket leaves Henry II and Louis VII, all parties gesticulating furiously. English manuscript illumination from the *Becket Leaves*, *c.* 1250.

rival, the Archbishop of York. Becket was incensed by this violation of the privileges of the See of Canterbury, and obtained from the Pope the suspension of the Archbishop of York and the excommunication of the Bishops of London and Salisbury, who had assisted him at the coronation.

With the King's consent Becket eventually returned to England on 1 December 1170, landing at Sandwich, then a major port at the mouth of the River Stour on the Kentish coast. Arriving in Canterbury, where he was received by the people with great rejoicing, he went barefoot through the streets to the Cathedral. There he gave every monk a kiss of peace and preached in the Chapter House. Meanwhile he had sent the documents of suspension and excommunication to the three prelates, who appealed immediately to the King, then celebrating Christmas with his court in Normandy. Henry ranted and raged, cursing his court as a nest of cowards, none of whom would rid him of this low-born priest. At this prompting, four knights (Reginald fitzUrse, Hugh de Morville, William de Tracy and Richard le Breton) decided to enforce what they believed to be the King's will. Crossing the Channel to England by separate routes, they arrived at Saltwood Castle, near Hythe. The castle, though technically part of the Archbishop's domains, had, during his exile in France, been given to Becket's bitter enemy, Randolph de Broc. Once there, the knights determined their strategy, and early on the morning of 29 December 1170, accompanied by a few retainers, they set out along Stone Street, the ancient Roman road from Lymme to Canterbury.

Late in the afternoon the knights were admitted to the Archbishop's chamber at the eastern end of the great hall adjoining the Cathedral. After an angry altercation they went to recover the swords they had left beneath a mulberry tree in the courtyard. On returning to the great hall and finding the entrance barred to them, they gained access through an upper window where workmen were doing repairs and made again for the Archbishop's chamber. By then, however, Becket had left, having been persuaded by his anxious servants to seek sanctuary in the Cathedral.

Accompanied by a few monks and clerks and preceded by his archiepiscopal cross, Becket walked slowly and calmly from the great hall to the Cathedral by means of a little-used passage leading through the cellarer's range into the cloisters. It used to be thought that the small group entered the cloisters at the north-west corner and moved along the northern and eastern alleys of the cloisters, halting for a moment at the Chapter House. But recent evidence cited by Professor Barlow suggests that the more likely route, taken also by the pursuing knights and their attendants, was along the southern alley closest to the great hall. No doors barred the way of the knights, Becket having refused to allow any to be locked behind him. By now he knew his fate, and wished to do nothing to frustrate it.

Upon entering the Cathedral through the Chapel of St Benedict in the north-west transept, the Archbishop moved to the steps leading towards the choir. He may have been making for the high altar, or perhaps St Augustine's chair in which he had been consecrated Archbishop eight years earlier. Hearing his entry, the monks singing vespers in the choir broke off their chanting and came to greet their Archbishop with relief; but Becket bade them return to their worship. He began to mount the

The southern alley of the cloisters, along which Becket probably walked to his murder.

The coronation of the young Henry III on 14 June 1170 by Roger of Pont l'Evêque, the Archbishop of York; right: Henry serves his son at the coronation banquet in Westminster (from the *Becket Leaves*).

Above right: Henry II is confronted by Becket while soldiers wait in the background; a 14th-century English manuscript illumination.

Below right: The four knights arrive at the Archbishop's Palace while Becket dines; from the first known miniature of the martyrdom, painted in England *c.* 1180.

Thomas's arrival at Sandwich on 1 December 1170; the sick are carried out to meet his ship while a small crowd, including some soldiers and a bishop, awaits him on the shore (from the *Becket Leaves*).

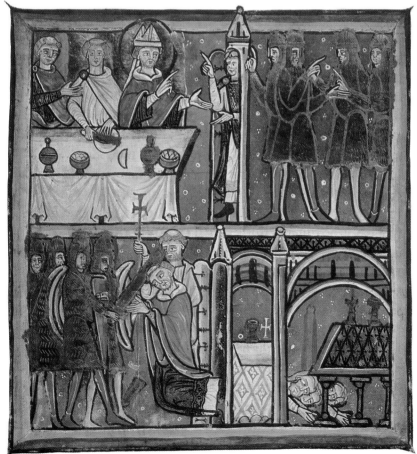

The door leading from the south-east corner of the cloisters into the north-west transept of the cathedral – the site of Becket's martyrdom.

Right: Plan of the cathedral showing the probable route taken by Becket and the knights.

steps to the high altar. It was now about five o'clock, and the darkness of the transept was relieved only by the lamp on the altar of St Benedict. What happened next is clear in general terms though not in detail. Several contemporary accounts exist, though they differ in detail and sometimes in substance. The following description of the tragedy that was to shake the whole of Europe is drawn from the narrative of William fitzStephen, a clerk attending the Archbishop who was, by his own account, a witness to the murder.[2]

The knights and their attendants rushed into St Benedict's Chapel

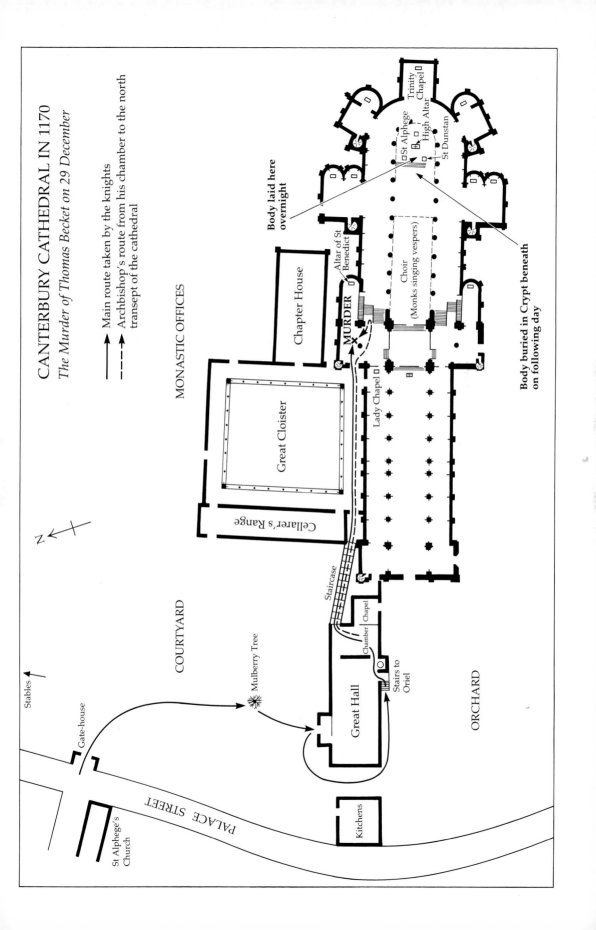

CANTERBURY CATHEDRAL IN 1170
The Murder of Thomas Becket on 29 December

⟶ Main route taken by the knights

⇢ Archbishop's route from his chamber to the north transept of the cathedral

N

MONASTIC OFFICES

Chapter House

Great Cloister

Cellarer's Range

Altar of St Benedict

MURDER

Lady Chapel

Choir (Monks singing vespers)

Staircase

Chamber | Chapel

Great Hall

Stairs to Oriel

Mulberry Tree

COURTYARD

Stables

Gate-house

ORCHARD

Kitchens

St Alphege's Church

PALACE STREET

Body laid here overnight

St Alphege

High Altar

St Dunstan

Trinity Chapel

Body buried in Crypt beneath on following day

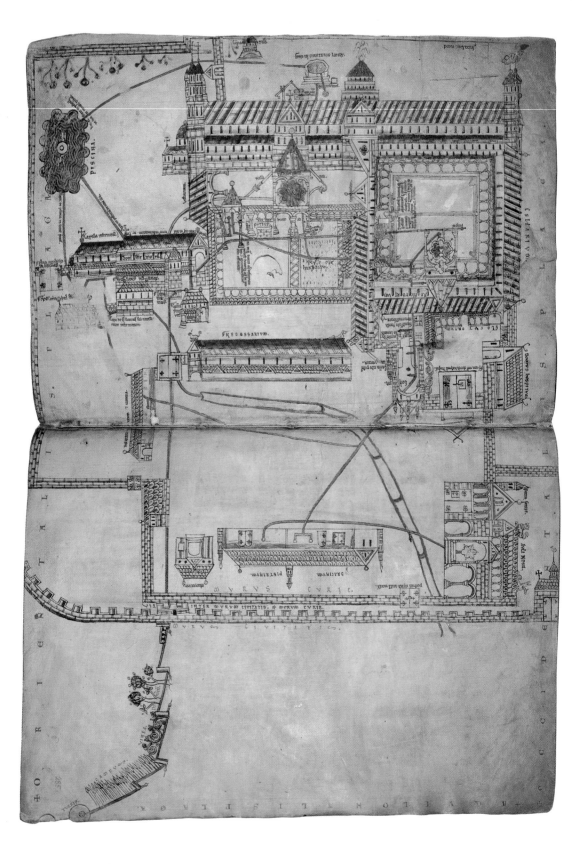

The news of the martyrdom travelled throughout Christendom. This late 12th-century fresco in the church of SS. Giovanni e Paolo in Spoleto depicts the moment when Edward Grim raised his arm to protect Becket from the fatal blow.

Left: Plan of the cloisters and the cathedral, from the 'waterworks plan', the only surviving depiction of the cathedral and priory as it was in Becket's time.

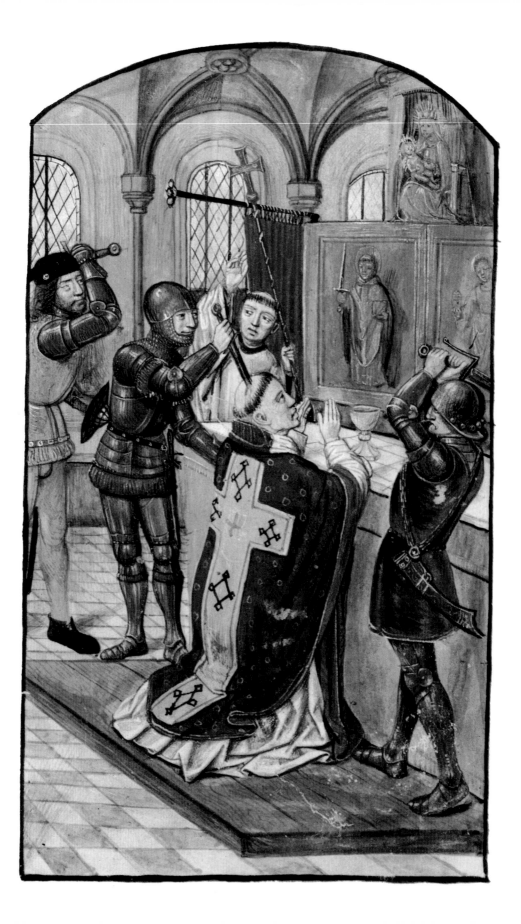

from the cloisters, in pursuit of Becket. One cried, 'Where is the Archbishop?' Becket answered, 'Here I am, no traitor but a priest of God, and I marvel that you have entered the church of God in such attire. What do you want with me?' One of the knights replied, 'That you should die: you cannot live any longer'. Then Becket said, 'I accept death in the name of the Lord, and I commend my soul and the cause of the church to God.'

Another knight then struck the Archbishop between his shoulders with the flat of his sword, saying, 'Fly, you are a dead man.' Becket stood unmoved, and, offering his head for a blow, continued to commend his soul to God. One of the knights said, 'You are a prisoner, come with us.' Seizing Becket, he tried to drag him from the Cathedral; but he was afraid that the townspeople, who were assembling outside in readiness for evensong in the nave, would rescue him. Becket said, 'I will not leave; here shall you work your will and obey your orders.'

At this, William de Tracy brandished his sword over Becket's head, preparing to strike the first blow. Upon seeing this Edward Grim, a secular clerk attending the Archbishop, raised his arm to protect Becket and took the force of the blow, suffering a severe wound. The same blow also struck Becket on his bowed head, drawing blood. He wiped away the blood with his sleeve, saying, 'Into thy hands, O Lord, I commend my spirit.' A second blow landed, causing him to fall first on his knees and then on his face, with his hands joined and stretched out to God. As he lay there, Richard le Breton struck a blow to his head of such force that the sword broke on the pavement.

The Archbishop received four strokes, all to the head, and the whole crown of his head was cut off. Then Hugh of Horsea, the chaplain to Randolph de Broc, otherwise known as Hugh Mauclerc, planted his foot on Becket's neck, and with the point of his sword drew out the blood and brains from the gash of the severed crown, scattering them on the pavement. 'Let us go, knights,' he said. 'This fellow will not rise again.' The knights and their attendants hastily retreated.

For a long time Becket lay almost alone in the darkness, forsaken by the monks and clerks. Eventually his chamberlain, Osbert, cut off a strip of his shirt to cover the remains of the half-severed head. As soon as they realised that the knights had left, the monks and clerks, together with their servants, came back to the dead Archbishop. A crowd of people from Canterbury entered the Cathedral and swarmed around him. Cries of lamentation and grief filled the air, continuing for much of the night. At length the monks decided to cover and bind the martyr's cracked skull with a clean linen cloth. The body was placed on a bier and carried through the choir to the high altar, where it lay for the

One of the knights plunges his sword into Becket's head; again Grim is shown with his arm raised; a Flemish miniature, *c.* 1500.

remainder of the night between the shrines of two of Becket's saintly predecessors, Alphege and Dunstan.

Some of the monks, among them Ernold the goldsmith, returned to the place of the assassination and carefully scooped into a basin the brains and blood that had been spilt on to the pavement. They placed benches across the site to prevent it being trampled by those coming and going past it. Throughout the night, watch was kept in the Cathedral in a sober, pious and holy fashion, the silence being disturbed only by the monks reciting the office for the commendation of a departed soul.

The following morning a rumour spread that members of the household of Randolph de Broc, in whose castle at Saltwood the four knights had stayed the night before the attack, regretted that the murder had taken place inside the Cathedral and were planning to drag the body outside. Fearful of this intention, the monks hastily began their preparations for the burial. They decided not to wash or embalm the body, for (as men reflected later) it had already been bathed in Becket's own blood. His outer clothes were removed and portioned out, but the hair-shirt and sackcloth drawers that he was found to be wearing were left on him, together with his shoes and monk's habit. He was then clothed in the vestments he had worn on the day of his consecration – the alb, pall, chrismatic, mitre, stole and maniple.

Thus clothed, the Archbishop's body was carried to the crypt beneath the choir and placed in a new marble coffin that, almost miraculously, happened to be there. On top of his body were laid the insignia of his office – his tunicle, dalmatic, chasuble, pallium, chalice, gloves, ring, sandals and pastoral staff. No mass was said, for the Cathedral had been desecrated by the intrusion of the armed knights, but the burial rites were performed. Then, amid tears of grief, the coffin was interred in the small and remote rectangular Chapel of the Holy Trinity at the extreme eastern end of the crypt, between the twin altars of St John the Baptist and St Augustine of Canterbury.

At this point fitzStephen's narrative ends; but the story continues in the writings of Gervase and Benedict, two monks of the Priory of Christ Church at Canterbury at the time of the martyrdom.[3] The doors of the crypt in which Becket's body had been buried were bolted and barred for more than three months, but in April 1171 they were opened to admit the public. At once the burial site became associated with miraculous cures, which gained in number and power with the passage of time. Many are beautifully and dramatically depicted in the richly coloured thirteenth-century stained-glass windows in the Trinity Chapel – the so-called 'miracle windows'. Angered by the dead Archbishop's waxing reputation for miracles of healing, his enemies once again threatened to

Becket's consecration as Archbishop of Canterbury on 3 June 1162; a marginal illustration from Queen Mary's Psalter, early 14th century.

seize his body and carry it away. One night, fearing an imminent swoop, the monks removed the body from its marble coffin, placed it in a wooden chest, and hid it for a while behind the altar of Our Lady in the Undercroft in another part of the crypt. Later they may have moved it to the apse of St Gabriel's Chapel, on the south side of the crypt, which, as Gervase had noted, was closed off at about this time.[4]

Even this, it seems, failed to dull the miraculous powers of the saint. Benedict tells the story of Richard, son of Eilnold of Bearstead, hardly able to walk, who came to the grave believing it still to contain Becket's body. Uncontrollably, he was drawn by a mysterious force towards the altar behind which the chest had been hidden. There, after prostrating himself in adoration, he began to leap about in a way that would have taxed the strength and agility even of a robust man.

When the danger of theft had passed and Becket's body had been returned to its original site of burial in the Chapel of the Holy Trinity, the monks decided to protect the body from the risk of further violation by surmounting the grave with a sort of tomb. It consisted of four strong

16

walls, constructed of stone and compacted with mortar, lead and iron. A huge slab was placed on top of the walls. Two oval apertures were left in each side wall through which pilgrims could place their hands, heads, or in some cases their whole bodies to be closer to the coffin. Many depictions of the tomb, with its oval openings, can still be seen in the 'miracle windows' in the Trinity Chapel, and similar tombs survive of St Osmond in Salisbury Cathedral and St Candida in Whitchurch Canonicorum, Dorset. Thereafter the grave in the crypt appears to have been secure.

Thomas Becket was canonised as St Thomas of Canterbury on 21 February 1173. The following year, on 12 July 1174, King Henry II did penance at the tomb, having walked barefoot and meanly clothed to the Cathedral from the church of St Dunstan, a little to the north-west of Canterbury. Upon entering the Cathedral he went to the place of the martyrdom and kissed the sacred stone where Becket had fallen. He then moved to the burial site in the crypt, laid his cloak aside, and knelt in front of the tomb, placing his head through one of the oval apertures in the side wall. Having received five strokes of a rod from each of the bishops and abbots present and three strokes from each of the eighty monks, he spent the whole night fasting in the crypt.

Barely three months later, on 5 September 1174, much of the choir of the Cathedral to the east of the central tower was destroyed in a great fire.[5] It began in the afternoon and was caused by sparks from a burning thatch in the nearby Burgate Street being carried by the wind to the roof of the choir. Engulfed by the flames that were fanned by a stiff south-easterly breeze, the wooden roof eventually succumbed to the fire, crashing down on to the woodwork in the choir below. Flames shot up to a great height, damaging the stone walls and columns of the Cathedral and spreading to some of the nearby buildings of the priory. Yet the tomb of Becket, in the crypt beneath the devastated choir, survived the conflagration unharmed; and, protected by a wooden shelter, it continued to attract its streams of pilgrims throughout the years in which the rebuilding of the eastern end of the Cathedral was proceeding around and above it.

The work of rebuilding was entrusted first to a Frenchman, William of Sens, and, after he had been incapacitated by a fall from the vaulting of the half-completed choir in 1178, to an English builder known only as William the Englishman. The monks, needing to provide a more glorious resting place for the relics of their martyred saint, resolved that the reconstructed Cathedral should culminate at its eastern end in a soaring, spacious chapel (the new Trinity Chapel), designed to be the setting for a wondrous new shrine in which the holy remains would eventually

17

The altar of Our Lady in the Undercroft, in the western crypt. It was behind this altar that Becket's body was for temporary protection placed soon after his death.

rest. After clearing the debris from the fire, rebuilding began in the following year (1175). As the reconstruction proceeded eastwards from the central tower, the building plans were changed to create an almost theatrical approach to the great Trinity Chapel in which the shrine was to stand. Huge, twisting flights of steps were built in the north and south choir aisles to take the pilgrims on an ever-rising path from the site of the martyrdom in the north-west transept to the choir, and from there to the Trinity Chapel itself where the glistening shrine of the saint would rise into view like a great ship of state.

In order to support the new Trinity Chapel, an extension had to be built to the crypt beneath it, for although the original Norman crypt in which Becket was buried had survived the fire, it fell short in length of

18

The openings in the shrine of St Candida, Whitchurch Canonicorum, Dorset, allowed pilgrims closer access to the relics housed within it.

the eastern extremity of the new choir being built above it. Work on the eastern extension of the crypt, under the direction of William the Englishman, began in 1179. The Chapel of the Holy Trinity, in which the tomb of Becket stood, was cleared away and the tomb itself was covered with a protective wooden shelter. The new eastern crypt, which is the one that exists today, was of an early Gothic style never before seen in England, with slender columns, rounded abacuses, moulded vaulting ribs and pointed arches. On its completion in 1181, Becket's tomb was located in the central aisle between the easternmost two of three dark Purbeck marble columns supporting the stone vaulting of the roof. It stood almost exactly beneath the place where, in the new Trinity Chapel above, his shrine was to be placed. Overlooking the tomb, high above the entrance arch to the eastern crypt, two windows were built into a small chamber beneath the high altar of the Cathedral, enabling the monks at all times to keep a watchful eye on the precious site.

During the ensuing years many pilgrims, both great and lowly, came to the tomb. Among the notable visitors were King Henry II (on several occasions following his penitential visit in 1174), his son Henry, the Dean of Chartres, the Earls of Flanders and of Essex, the Archbishops of Rheims, Lyons and Cologne, King Louis VII of France, King William of Scotland, King Richard I of England (*en route* to Dover for the crusades), and an Icelandic Chief named Rajn Sveinbjarnarson. King John and Queen Isabella were crowned in the Cathedral by Archbishop Walter in 1201, and they would doubtless have made a pilgrimage down to the tomb in the recently completed eastern crypt.

As the major attraction for pilgrims visiting Canterbury during the late twelfth and early thirteenth centuries, the tomb of St Thomas Becket yielded a substantial income for the Priory of Christ Church. In 1179 King Louis VII of France gave a cup of pure gold, a huge ruby known as the Régale of France, and an annual allowance of about 1,600 gallons of wine. Most of the offerings, however, were from ordinary pilgrims. In 1207, monetary gifts at the tomb amounted to £320, although the sums in later years varied considerably. In 1213, during the period of the banishment of the priory by King John, the amount was only £60 17s.[6]

By 1220, the fiftieth anniversary of the martyrdom, the rebuilding of the eastern part of the Cathedral following the great fire of 1174 was complete, and the stage was set for the transfer (or, as it was known, the 'translation') of Becket's remains from their relatively humble tomb in the eastern crypt to the magnificent new shrine in the Trinity Chapel above. Several narratives exist of the event; the following account is based upon the *Polistorie*, a Canterbury chronicle in French that is generally regarded as bearing the stamp of accuracy.

The day of the translation (7 July 1220) was both a great religious ceremony of deep solemnity and an enormous and probably riotous public festival. It had been two years in the planning, and was attended by the young King (Henry III) together with archbishops, bishops, abbots, priors and magnates from all over Europe. There were so many visitors that the houses in Canterbury and in the surrounding suburbs and villages were full to overflowing, and tents had to be erected in the surrounding fields. The day was hot and wine was distributed free of

Miracles performed at Becket's shrine, depicted in stained glass at Canterbury Cathedral, from a 13th-century window.

Thomas Becket, Archbishop of Canterbury. A very early portrait from a 13th-century window in the Trinity Chapel.

charge from barrels provided by Archbishop Stephen Langton at each gate leading into the city.

Inside the Cathedral, the proceedings were more reverent and decorous. On the evening of 6 July Archbishop Langton and Prior Walter, accompanied by all the monks of the priory, assembled at the tomb of St Thomas in the eastern crypt where, having prayed, they opened the coffin. The solemn and moving event is recounted in the *Polistorie* in the following words.

> Then were the stones of the tomb removed without injury by the hands of the monks appointed thereunto, and the others all rose up and drew near, and gazing upon the martyr they could not restrain their tears for joy. And then once more they all applied themselves to prayers in common, except certain monks who were specially chosen for their holy living to remove that precious treasure out of the sepulchre. These lifted him and put him in a seemly wooden chest, adorned for the purpose, the which was well strengthened with iron, and they fastened it also carefully with iron nails, and then carried him to a seemly and secret place, until they should celebrate solemnly on the morrow the day of the translation.
>
> Then in the morning all the prelates assembled themselves in the mother church, to wit Pandulf, legate of the holy church of Rome, and Stephen, Archbishop of Canterbury, with all the other bishops, his suffragans, who were come, save three, of whom one was dead, and two were excused by reason of sickness. These went forthwith to the place where the glorious martyr abode, in the presence of the King of England, Henry III, and the prelates thereto appointed devoutly took the chest on their shoulders, and carried it into the choir before the altar of the Trinity. There they put him honourably with all reverence under another wooden chest very richly adorned with gold and precious stones.[7]

A somewhat different account is given in another source known as the *Quadrilogus* – a thirteenth-century conflation of five separate biographies of Becket.[8] According to this account, the body was removed from the coffin in the crypt on 27 June – several days before its translation to the shrine in the Trinity Chapel. The body was first taken by several of the monks and given to the Archbishop, who himself placed it in a 'feretrum', or iron container, having first reserved a few small bones for distribution to great men and famous churches. The feretrum was then fastened with iron nails and carried by the monks to a bier in an honourable place, where it rested until the ceremony of the translation on 7

The pilgrim steps leading from the south choir aisle to the Trinity Chapel. As they climbed these steps, pilgrims would have had their first glimpse of the shrine of St Thomas.

Above and below: Miracles occuring at Becket's tomb in the crypt; from 13th-century stained glass in the Trinity Chapel.

July. A similar story is told in the *Icelandic Saga of Thomas*, an early fourteenth-century biography of Becket based on Robert of Cricklade's life of the saint.[9] According to the *Saga*, the body of the saint crumbled to dust when it was removed from the coffin (which would be expected if it had not been embalmed), and what was placed in the feretrum was not a body but a collection of bones. The *Icelandic Saga* corroborated the evidence of the *Quadrilogus* that a number of small bones were kept aside for later distribution.

Of the shrine itself, nothing remains except some traces of stonework in the floor of the Trinity Chapel.[10] Two complete images of the shrine exist, one in a medallion in a thirteenth-century miracle window in the Trinity Chapel, the other a much later sixteenth-century drawing in the Cottonian Manuscripts in the British Library.[11] There are also partial images in another window of the Trinity Chapel, and what might be a rough representation is visible in a window in the north choir aisle of the Cathedral depicting the story of Noah and the flood. In addition, several descriptions of the shrine appear in sixteenth-century chronicles, including an eye witness account of it given by the European scholar Erasmus during a visit to the Cathedral in about 1512,[12] which seem to have been used as the basis for the drawing in the Cottonian Manuscripts.

The shrine, upon which no expense was spared in its construction, was the work of two clerical craftsmen, Walter of Colchester and Elyas of Dereham. It was raised up on steps and fronted by an altar and consisted of three parts: a stone plinth with an open arcaded base, the richly gilded and decorated wooden casket in which the feretrum containing the relics of the saint was laid, and a painted wooden canopy, suspended from the roof by a series of pulleys that enabled it to be raised or lowered to reveal or cover the casket itself. The casket was covered in gold plate and decorated with fine golden trellis-work. Affixed to the gold plate were innumerable jewels, pearls, sapphires, diamonds, rubies and emeralds, together with rings and cameos of sculptured agates, cornelians and onyx stones. Also attached to the casket was the great Régale of France which King Louis VII had given at the tomb in the crypt in 1179. Writing of his visit to the Cathedral, Erasmus said of the shrine that 'the least valuable portion was of gold, but every part glistened, shone, and sparkled with rare and very large jewels, some of them larger than a goose's egg'.[13]

The spectacle of the shrine in the magnificent Gothic setting of the Trinity Chapel must have been awesome to generations of medieval pilgrims. After making their way to the Trinity Chapel from the site of the martyrdom and the crypt, many of them crawling on their hands and

An artist's impression of Becket's shrine before its destruction in 1538.

knees and prostrating themselves before the shrine, the climactic moment came for the canopy to be raised on its pulleys and the glistening casket revealed. According to Erasmus's narrative, silver bells tinkled and one of the officers of the priory came forward with a white wand, touching the many jewels with it, indicating their quality and value, and naming their donors. After prayers and intercessions had been offered and gifts surrendered, the canopy descended and the

26

pilgrims withdrew from the Trinity Chapel down the opposite flight of steps from that by which they had ascended.

What the pilgrims did not see, of course, were the actual remains of Becket. These were safely contained within the feretrum, in which they had been placed by Archbishop Stephen Langton and the monks during the ceremony in the crypt in 1220. There appears to be no exact record of the relics that were placed in the feretrum, or how they were arranged, and this compounds the difficulty of unravelling their fate in 1538. Two statements can, however, be made with some certainty. First, there are no grounds for believing that the bones placed in the shrine were other than those of Becket. Secondly, it seems clear that what was laid in the feretrum was not a body but a set of bones. It is true that the language of both the *Polistorie* and the *Quadrilogus* is suggestive of a body; but the *Icelandic Saga of Thomas* is very clear about the disintegration of the tissues of the body upon being touched. Moreover, the *Saga* speaks explicitly of 'laying the bones into the chest', and both it and the *Quadrilogus* record the fact that Archbishop Langton kept a few bones back for later distribution – an action that could hardly have happened if the body had somehow been preserved intact.

The drawing of the shrine in the Cottonian Manuscripts differs in a number of respects from the depiction of it in the miracle window in the Trinity Chapel, and is generally thought to be the less reliable of the two.[14] After all, the representation in the Trinity Chapel window could have been seen by the pilgrims merely by raising their eyes from the real thing, and any obvious dissimilarities would have been noticed by those with sufficiently good eyesight to observe the detail. Nevertheless, the Cottonian drawing is interesting for two reasons. First, it seems to confirm that the shrine contained a set of bones, not a body. The inscription beneath the drawing was partially destroyed by fire in 1731, but it can be reconstructed from the late sixteenth-century annals of John Stow (see Chapter 7) from which it was probably taken. It reads:

> This chest of iron contained the bones of Thomas Becket, skull and all, with the wounde of his death and the pece cut out of his skull laid in the same wounde.[15]

The second interesting feature of the Cottonian drawing is its representation of the arrangement of the bones within the feretrum. It is not clear whether the representation was actually painted on the canopy of the shrine (and if so, whether it purported to be an accurate statement of how the bones were really arranged), or whether it derived only from the imagination of the artist who produced the drawing. What it shows

A representation of the shrine survives in this 13th-century stained glass from the Trinity Chapel. It shows a vision of St Thomas emerging from the shrine.

Left: The Trinity Chapel: looking north-east across the site of Becket's shrine to the tomb of the first Dean of Canterbury, Nicholas Wootton.

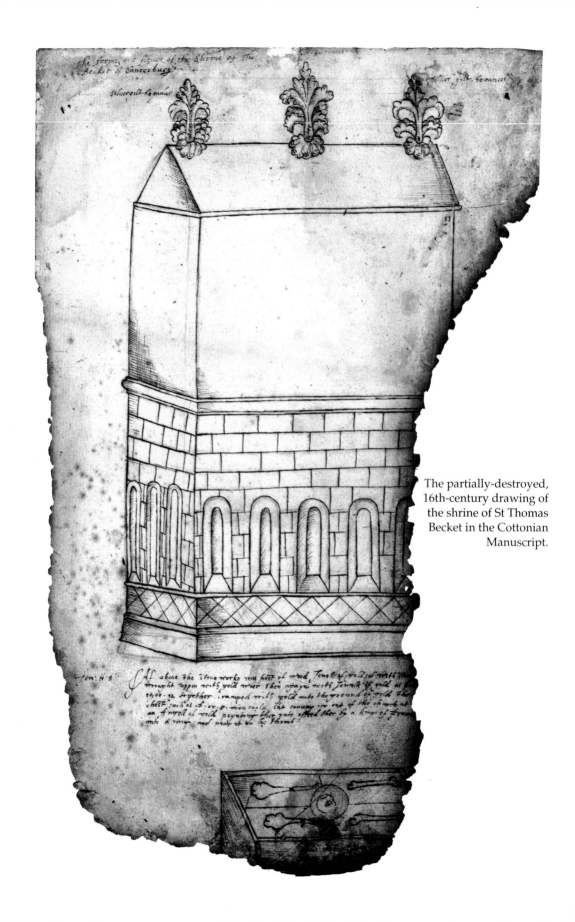

The partially-destroyed, 16th-century drawing of the shrine of St Thomas Becket in the Cottonian Manuscript.

is an arrangement of bones not in the rough shape of a skeleton but in a rectangular pattern around the skull, which is placed in the centre. This arrangement is instructive in view of the way in which the bones may have been arranged in the coffin that was discovered in the eastern crypt in 1888 (see Chapter 2).

From 1220 onwards the shrine in the Trinity Chapel superseded the tomb in the crypt as the major attraction for the multitudes of pilgrims flocking to Canterbury. This is confirmed in the records that exist of the sums of money offered each year at the various sites in the Cathedral associated with St Thomas: the shrine, the place of the martyrdom, the tomb in the crypt, and the corona at the eastern end of the Trinity Chapel where something purporting to be part of Becket's skull was shown to pilgrims. In most years until 1220, the tomb in the crypt attracted the greatest volume of offerings; thereafter the shrine obviously predominated. By the end of the thirteenth century the offerings at the tomb had all but dried up, although the empty tomb itself continued to stand on an altar-like plinth between the Purbeck marble columns in the eastern crypt until it suffered the same fate as the shrine at the hands of the King's Commissioners in 1538. Parts of the walls of the tomb are said to have been used in the repair of the pavement surrounding the central aisle in this part of the crypt. They are still visible, embedded with other stones and slabs in the ancient flooring.

Long before then, however, the cult of Becket had begun to wane, having perhaps been almost the victim of its own success. The reverence attached to his memory had become exaggerated beyond reasonable proportion, and the genuinely religious purposes of many pilgrims in visiting the shrine were matched by others of a much more dubious kind. Devotion became mingled with superstition and deception as the custodians of the major sites endeavoured to extract the maximum offerings from pilgrims. Nowhere is the flavour of uncritical veneration and superstitious decadence better captured than in the precisely observed account left by the great European scholar Erasmus, who visited the Cathedral in about 1512 in the company of a leading English scholar, John Colet, Dean of St Paul's.[16]

Erasmus was plainly impressed by the beauty of the building and the compelling simplicity of some of the plainer memorials to Becket, particularly the small wooden altar in the site of the martyrdom. The ostentatious wealth of the place oppressed him, however, as did the endless array of relics that were brought out for his and Colet's veneration. Erasmus commented on the 'astonishing quantity' of skulls, jaws, teeth, hands, fingers and arms that they were shown, and described the custodian who produced these wares as a 'showman'. Other relics

John Colet, Dean of St Paul's, kneeling before St Matthew, in a manuscript illumination by Peter Meghen.

elicited the positive disgust of the two visitors: there is no mistaking the revulsion of Colet over the arm, still with flesh attached, that he was invited to kiss, or the scraps of handkerchiefs he was given to touch, soiled by 'the sweat from the face or neck of the saint, the running of his nose, and things of that sort'. Colet fingered them with deep distaste before laying them contemptuously aside. The prior, like a dull man, pretended not to see, and offered them a glass of wine.

The English Reformation, when it came, was in certain respects perhaps long overdue. In Canterbury, as elsewhere, it had as one of its objectives the suppression of the monasteries and the elimination of the superstitious veneration of relics that had so offended Erasmus and Colet. Acting under the authority of the Lord Privy Seal, Thomas Cromwell, the King's Commissioners embarked upon a huge and furious purge of all the symbols of the old and objectionable practices. Throughout 1537 and 1538, in the greatest ever pillage of medieval artwork, the cathedrals of England were literally ransacked of all their finest treasures.[17] The spectacular shrines and their coverings were demolished, monuments were pulled down, statues were smashed, and the huge collections of saintly relics (over 400 items in Canterbury

32

Cathedral alone) were destroyed or otherwise dispersed. Nothing was to be left that could act as a visible focus of continuing veneration.

In Canterbury, where the greatest and most celebrated of all the shrines of England was standing, the destruction had a deeper purpose. St Thomas Becket was not simply a saint like the rest. His particular and despicable crime, in the eyes of King Henry VIII, had been his challenge to the authority of his royal predecessor, Henry II, and he was the greatest of the English martyrs. His was a special case requiring, perhaps, special treatment. In September 1538 the Royal Commissioners for the Destruction of Shrines, headed by Dr Richard Layton, Archdeacon of Buckingham, arrived in Canterbury to do their business.[18] The shrine was demolished, along with those of several other saints whose remains had been kept at Canterbury, and the vast hoard of gold and jewels was carried off to the King's coffers in London. The bones of St Thomas were removed from the feretrum in which they had rested for over 318 years.

Becket goes into exile in France in 1164; marginal illumination from Queen Mary's Psalter.

2   The Skeleton in the Crypt

T he bones that were found in the eastern crypt of Canterbury Cathedral on Monday 23 January 1888 were uncovered in the course of an archaeological investigation commissioned by the Dean and Chapter. It was stressed by those responsible for the investigation that its aim was simply to find the eastern extremities of an earlier Norman Cathedral built in the latter part of the eleventh century. There was, according to the Cathedral authorities, no question of hunting around for bones. Accounts of the find appeared in correspondence in *The Times* in February and March 1888 and in two reports presented to the Dean and Chapter that were subsequently published in a local historical journal, *Archaeologia Cantiana*. The first report, dated 28 April 1888, was written by the three-man committee appointed by the Dean and Chapter to carry out the archaeological investigation: Canon Charles F. Routledge, Dr J. Brigstock Sheppard and Canon W.A. Scott Robertson.[1] The second report, comprising the results of a medical examination of the bones, was written by Mr W. Pugin Thornton, a local surgeon called in to inspect them.[2]

The bones were contained in a coffin buried just below the surface in the eastern crypt, between the western most two of the three Purbeck marble pillars in the central aisle. Immediately to the east of this place (that is, between the two easternmost of the three pillars) a hollowed-out space was found, extending to about three feet beneath the surface, filled with rubble. It was in this place that Becket's body had been buried for fifty years from 1170 to 1220; and the committee thought that the hollowed-out space was probably the actual grave in which the marble coffin had lain. Two long, thin steps of Purbeck marble were also uncovered nearby, which the committee identified as those leading to the altar where the tomb had stood until its destruction in 1538. The coffin containing the bones was therefore lying in a place most intimately associated with Becket – a mere few feet away from the site of his erstwhile tomb, and almost exactly beneath the place in the Trinity Chapel above where his shrine had once stood.

The coffin was said to have been buried no more than three inches beneath the level of the floor, which at that time was only bare earth.[3]

The site in the eastern crypt where the grave was discovered in 1888. Beyond it, between the two Purbeck marble pillars, was the place of Becket's first burial from 1170 to 1220.

The coffin was six feet and two inches long, hewn out of a solid block of Portland oolite and covered with a thin slab of Merstham or Reigate firestone. The committee expressed the view that the covering slab was 'utterly unfitted for such a purpose'.[4] Further evidence of the unusual nature of the coffin was the fact that its width at the widest point was a mere fifteen inches, suggesting that it would more accurately be described as a rough stone coffer than as a coffin.[5] An elderly Cathedral workman who tried to lie down in it was unable to do so;[6] nor could Mr Thornton, the surgeon who examined the bones.[7] The coffin itself was not removed from the ground, and the earth beneath it was not excavated.[8] Had this been done, it is possible that one or even two additional coffins might have been found beneath it. The reasons for this seemingly bizarre statement are examined in Chapter 8.

None of the three members of the committee actually witnessed the uncovering of the coffin. Indeed, they did not see it until part of the lid had been removed. Their report did not indicate the length of time that had elapsed before they viewed the coffin, but they noted that by then the lid had broken into two parts. They were unable to say whether the damage to the lid had been sustained before the excavation began or during the course of it, and they seemingly failed to check the matter with those who had uncovered the coffin.

The coffin contained human bones, mixed with earth and other debris. The earth was carefully sifted,[9] but nothing other than the bones was reported as having been found. The bones were, according to the members of the committee, not placed in any regular order but were gathered together 'in a heap' near the middle and upper portion of the coffin. Other accounts of the state of the coffin, however, suggest otherwise. One eyewitness, Miss Holland, later described the bones as 'laid round the head in a sort of square',[10] and the surgeon, Mr Thornton, depicted them as being 'arranged somewhat in reverential order, the long bones lying across one another, similar to the position we arrange spears and swords on the walls of museums'.[11] At the head of the coffin was a boulder-like stone, hollowed on its upper surface as if to form a sort of pillow. It was broken across the middle. The committee reported that the bones made up the almost complete human skeleton of an adult of full stature and of at least middle age.

An account of the events surrounding the discovery has been left in the correspondence of Miss Agnes Holland, later Mrs Bolton.[12] She was the daughter of the Reverend F.J. Holland, Canon Residentiary of the Cathedral. Most of the letters are contemporary accounts of the find, written to Miss Lisa Rawlinson, the daughter of an Oxford professor. But one is a later letter, written in March 1915, in reply to questions put to her by Canon A.J. Mason, whose own crucial role in the story is set out in Chapter 5.[13]

In the letters Miss Holland recounts how, on hearing of the discovery, she went immediately to the crypt where she saw the bones before their removal from the coffin. Present at the time were one of the members of the committee (Canon Routledge), the Cathedral architect (Mr H.G. Austin), two workmen, and Miss Holland's father. Later the Bishop of Dover (Dr Parry), the Dean of Canterbury (Dr Robert Payne Smith), another member of the committee (Dr J.B. Sheppard), Miss Holland's mother, and others, arrived at the scene.

> I stood with them and looked down into the coffin. I perfectly remember the appearance of the skeleton. The great head lay on the slightly raised, hollowed-out, little stone pillow, and the bones were laid round the head in a sort of square. It gave a strange look. One saw the teeth.[14]

Miss Holland described how the bones were removed from the coffin, placed in a large box, and carried to the house in the precincts of the Cathedral architect, Mr Austin. There they lay in an unused room, on white deal boards covered with a grey cloth, beneath a pall of white silk. Two days later, on 25 January, they were shown to Mr Thornton, a member of the Royal College of Surgeons and an expert in the now discredited science of phrenology. He was involved at the behest of the Dean and Chapter,[15] possibly on account of his fame as a phrenologist, and he spent three days examining the bones. His findings, which were reported to the Dean and Chapter, were subsequently published.[16] Several years later he published a further pamphlet containing his own version of the events of January 1888.[17]

Thornton judged the bones to be very old, although he was unable to date them. He arranged the bones in anatomical order and mounted the several parts of the skull on a mound of damp modelling plaster. Several bones or parts of bones were missing, but the skeleton was, in Thornton's view, sufficiently complete to enable its broad features to be observed.

Thornton reported that the skeleton was that of an adult man, aged between about 45 and 55. By way of confirmation, Mr Luther Bell, a dental surgeon who examined the five teeth remaining in the skull, judged that death had occurred at about the age of 50. The bones of the body and limbs gave an impression of great height and strength: Thornton was of the opinion that the man had been more than six feet tall in life, 'probably six feet two inches'.

For obvious reasons, Thornton paid careful attention to the state of the

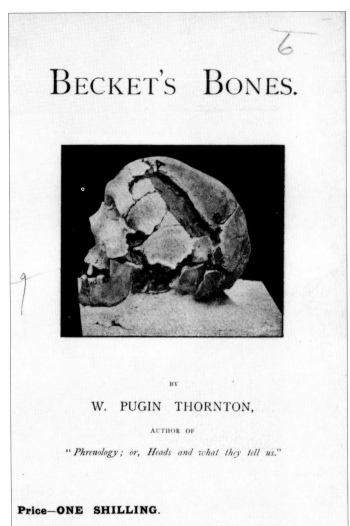

BECKET'S BONES.

BY

W. PUGIN THORNTON,

AUTHOR OF

"*Phrenology; or, Heads and what they tell us.*"

Price—ONE SHILLING.

The titlepage and (*right*) plates from Thornton's pamphlet *Becket's Bones* (1901). The photographs of the skull and skeleton were taken in 1888, when the grave in the eastern crypt was first uncovered.

skull. It was a large skull, some 22.75 inches in circumference, and its shape suggested to Thornton a man of 'large perceptive qualities, much intellect, indomitable energy, the power of arrangement and manage-ment, but unworthy of trust'.[18] The crown of the skull had sustained a very recent fracture, probably caused by the removal of the bones from the coffin. The right side of the skull had been fractured by a blow that, in Thornton's opinion, might have been caused by a mace or pickaxe, but not by a sword-cut. The left side of the skull had sustained a much greater injury: he noted in particular an aperture of five to six inches in

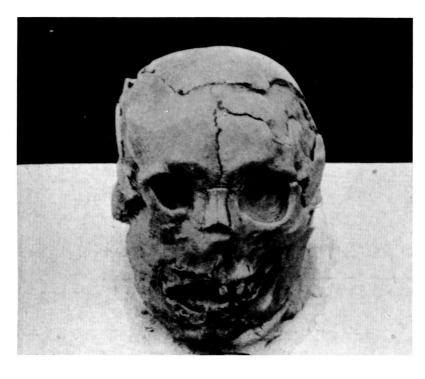

length extending from a line drawn upwards from behind the position of the ear to the centre of the forehead. Since the upper border of this aperture was in an almost straight line, Thornton concluded that, if the injury had resulted from force (either during life or after death), it might have been caused by a heavy cutting instrument such as a two-handed sword. Extending from the upper edge of this aperture was a crack in the skull of about 1.5 inches, which might have been caused during the man's lifetime.

Thornton's examination of, and report on, the bones and the skull provided much of the empirical evidence on which debate about their identity proceeded for the next sixty years or more. A great deal depended upon the accuracy of his observations and conclusions, the more so since the bones were fairly quickly reinterred, and few other experts had a similar chance to examine them. Yet it is clear from his report that Thornton's conduct of the examination was inadequate by modern scientific standards. Several measurements were given in approximate rather than precise quantities; one was quoted from memory, the written record having been lost; the personality and intelligence of the man was inferred solely from the size and shape of the skull; and unfounded assumptions were made about the likely causes of the injuries sustained by the skull. The report did not make clear which of the wounds in the skull had been caused in life and which in the process of extracting and removing it from the coffin. Moreover, it was not only Thornton's part in the process that, by modern standards, was flawed. The speed with which the bones were removed from the coffin, the failure to record their exact positions in the coffin before their removal, and the damage that was apparently caused to both the coffin and the bones would obviously be considered unacceptable in a contemporary archaeological excavation.

The bones were on the surface for sixteen days, during which time they were seen by a number of people. A Jesuit priest from London, Father John Morris, saw them on at least two occasions, and so too did Mr Aymer Vallance.[19] Miss Holland wrote in her letters of a man who came from Margate with his son.[20] He said that the boy's eyesight was failing, and that the doctors were unable to help. As a last resort, he wanted to see what the bones of the saint (whom he presumably believed to be Becket) could do for the boy. With the enthusiastic approval of Mr Austin, the Cathedral architect, the man made the boy kneel in front of the skull and place his eyes close to the orbital sockets, saying to him: 'Now, no doctors can heal you; you must pray for yourself.' To the attendant staff from the Cathedral he reportedly said: 'If this does not cure him, nothing will.'[21] The outcome is not recorded.

The removal and examination of the bones were not without criticism. A letter in *The Times* of 20 February 1888, signed simply 'An Englishman', complained of the irreverent and even sacrilegious behaviour of the Cathedral authorities:

> The Dean and Chapter and Mr Austin do not seem to have been aware that the unlawful removal of remains from consecrated ground – and surely it cannot be pretended that the reception rooms of Mr Austin's house stand on consecrated ground? – is not only a misdemeanour at common law, but a statutory offence. Further it should be borne in mind that the act has been done, not by a sacrilegious layman, but by the connivance and sanction of one of the most important ecclesiastical bodies in the kingdom – the Dean and Chapter of Canterbury.[22]

The bones were reinterred, in the grave from which they had been taken, at 3.30 p.m. on Friday, 10 February 1888.[23] The event was witnessed and recorded by the meticulous Miss Holland.

> Just as I arrived ... the little procession came in, Austin hurrying first and then the two workmen bearing between them the bier .... They laid the bier down beside the rough open coffin, and then proceeded to place in it ... a very nice strong oak shell, which exactly fitted .... Then Austin took the skull very carefully (still upon the clay mould) and laid it on the stone cushion ... and then Mr Thornton took his place, and receiving all the bones from Mr Austin laid them according to the latter's direction exactly in the position in which they were found, all neatly arranged in the upper part of the coffin .... Then Austin took up a glass bottle in which a photograph of the skull and a careful record of the finding had been sealed up, and asked the Dean if

The skeleton as photographed in 1888.

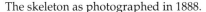

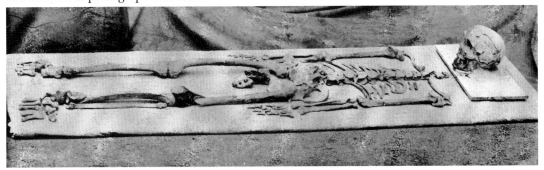

he was quite satisfied, and the Dean hurried to say 'Oh yes', and then the bottle was solemnly laid behind the head, and then the lid of oak was quickly screwed down by Andrews (the foreman of the Cathedral workmen), and we knew we had seen the last of our Saint – for be he St Thomas of Canterbury or not, he is some great and holy person. Then they cemented round the edge of the coffin and lowered down upon it a large new stone slab weighing 15 cwt. Then . . . the Dean assented to the proposition that the earth should be shovelled over it all again, and in five minutes every trace was hidden . . . I murmured softly in the Dean's ear, 'Mr Dean, wouldn't it be very nice if something was made to mark out the place? You know, tiles or something?' 'Oh yes. Something we will have.'[24]

This little ceremony, however, by no means signalled the end of the line for the skeleton in the crypt. Indeed, it merely marked the beginning of the extraordinary and ultimately mysterious chain of events that are narrated in the following chapters. The debate about the identification of the skeleton began on the very day of its reinterment (10 February 1888) with publication in *The Times* of the first letter in what was to become a lengthy and sometimes tetchy correspondence.

The burial of Thomas Becket; a manuscript
illumination from Alan of Tewkesbury's
collection of correspondence, *c.* 1180.

3   Believers, Agnostics and Sceptics

wo days after the discovery of the bones in the eastern crypt, on 25 January 1888, a new reredos was consecrated in St Paul's Cathedral, London.[1] Designed by G.F. Bodley, it was worked in marble and contained in its centre the largest crucifix to appear in an Anglican church since the Reformation. It was topped by a statue of the Virgin Mary. (The reredos was destroyed in the Second World War, though the statue still remains in the Cathedral.) Its appearance in 1888 disturbed the minds of many in the Protestant tradition who saw in its unaccustomed splendour yet further evidence of a shift within the Church of England towards Rome. The Oxford movement had by now reached the summit of its influence in the Church, and many of the Tractarian leaders in the earlier years of the movement had achieved high office. They included Dr R.W. Church, a close friend of John Henry Newman, who was appointed Dean of St Paul's in 1871, and Dr H.P. Liddon, an admirer of Edward Pusey, who became a canon of St Paul's in 1870. Royal patronage of the Anglo-Catholic wing of the Church of England followed these appointments, and relations with Rome were cordial. In 1887 Queen Victoria expressed her gratification at the Vatican's request for a papal envoy to be admitted at her jubilee celebrations that year, and later she dispatched the Duke of Norfolk on a mission to Rome to assure the Pope of her 'sincere friendship and unfeigned respect and esteem'.[2] In an age when the cry of 'no popery' could still arouse passion and fervour, deep concern was felt among the Protestant wing that a high church conspiracy might be afoot to transform England into a Roman Catholic nation.

Much of the tension between the Protestant and Anglo-Catholic sympathisers centred on matters of worship and doctrine, including a revival of interest in the issues of saintliness and martyrdom; but the steady and visible growth of ritual was also deplored by those who felt its incompatibility with the Protestant sentiment of the country. The use of incense, vestments and statues; the placing of lighted candles on the altar; the mixing of water with the wine and the cleansing of the vessels during the eucharist; the giving of the sign of the cross at the absolution and blessing; all these little acts of ritual, introduced as much at the discretion of individual clergy as through a deliberate act of high church defiance, were shocking to Protestant Anglicans. Ways had to be found of countering the threat.

In 1865 a group of Protestant churchmen formed the Church Association to resist these innovations. Though initially thwarted by the bishops in their attempts to have the ritualists prosecuted, they eventually managed to bring about the ecclesiastical trial of the saintly Bishop of Lincoln, Edward King, on a charge of ritual irregularity. The case came before the Archbishop of Canterbury's court and was heard in the library at Lambeth Palace. In his judgement in November 1890, the Archbishop (Edward White Benson) outlawed the sign of the cross at the blessing and absolution and also the mixing of water with the wine, but allowed the priest to turn eastwards during the consecration of the elements provided it did not obscure any 'manual acts' that might be performed.[3]

The turmoil over the quest for ritual order in the Church of England during the latter years of the nineteenth century created a climate of diverse and shifting tensions and loyalties. It led directly to the Royal Commission on Ecclesiastical Discipline of 1904–6, and ultimately to the stormy quest for a new Prayer Book in the 1920s (of which more will be said in Chapter 5). Within the hallowed precincts of the cathedrals, further difficulties arose in the latter years of the nineteenth century as a result of their parlous financial state, and questions were being asked about their function at a time when the parishes were rapidly expanding. As expenses rose and income fell, relationships between the cathedrals and the Ecclesiastical Commissioners were often fraught. In some places (including Winchester, Salisbury and Gloucester) the deans and canons drew only half their allowable stipends.[4] Canterbury was not immune to the general squeeze and uncertainty, which was exacerbated by the Commissioners' policy of diverting resources from the wealthier chapters towards the needs of the poorer churches in the dioceses.[5]

It is within this broad context that the significance of a skeleton found in Canterbury Cathedral, and thought perhaps to be that of the greatest of the English Catholic saints, should be understood. It is a context that helps to explain the speed with which the debate about the identity of the bones ensued, the intensity with which it was prosecuted, and the form it took. From the outset, even before any of the findings from the surgeon's examination of the skeleton were known, the question at issue was not 'Whose bones are they?', but 'Are they the bones of St Thomas Becket?' It was as though, from the moment of the discovery, the participants in the debate had made up their minds about the matter, and were using the apparent facts of the case not to form their opinions but to endorse conclusions they had already reached. Plainly, these were not just any old bones, indistinguishable from others that surface from time to time in ancient places. These were, potentially, very special bones, to be handled – metaphorically as well as literally – with great care.

It was clear almost from the beginning that several features of the discovery offered prima facie support for the possibility that the bones were those of Becket, which had been taken from the shrine at some time prior to its destruction in September 1538.

First, the coffin was unearthed from a hitherto unknown grave immediately adjacent to the site of Becket's tomb between 1170 and 1538, and almost directly beneath the spot where the shrine had stood in the Trinity Chapel between 1220 and 1538. It was, therefore, a place associated most intimately with Becket, and a seemingly unusual location for the burial of anyone else.

Section through the Corona, Trinity chapel and crypt.

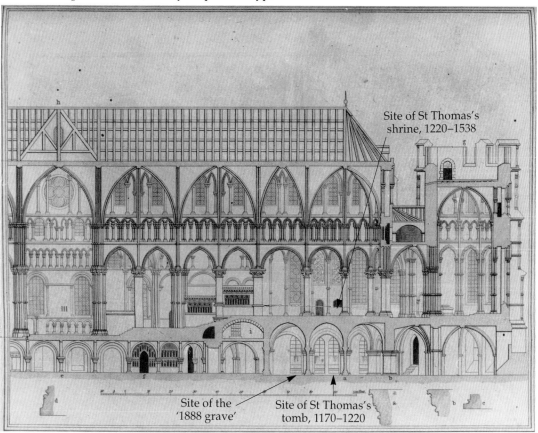

Secondly, the fact that the whole of the eastern crypt had been walled off in 1546 and given for use as a private cellar to the Bishop of Dover, Richard Thornden, suggested that the coffin had probably been interred at some time during the eight years or so following the final destruction of the tomb in 1538, after which any interment would have been unlikely in what was then a private building. Moreover, the fact that this part of the crypt remained until 1838 a private place and closed to the public would have protected the site from unwanted intruders and enquirers. Had any interment taken place after 1838, it would almost certainly have been known to the Cathedral authorities only fifty years later.

Thirdly, the ill-fitted nature of the coffin, with its narrow width, its unsuitable lid and its shallow depth of burial, suggested that the interment may have been a hasty one, using whatever container could rapidly be adapted for the purpose. This could be consistent with the proposition that, in 1538, the monks of Christ Church Priory had peremptorily retrieved Becket's remains from the shrine and buried them elsewhere in order to prevent their abuse by the King's Commissioners.

Fourthly, the positioning of the bones in the coffin – many of them collected together at one end, with some missing – showed that they had been placed in the coffin as a collection of bones, not as a body. Their interment had been an act of reburial, not of burial. In any case, the coffin would not have been large enough to accommodate the corpse of an adult man. If the bones were those of Becket, this would, of course, be consistent with the evidence reviewed in Chapter 1 that the tissues of Becket's body had disintegrated upon its removal from the original marble coffin in 1220, and that only his bones were placed in the shrine. Not only that, the absence of a few bones from the skeleton exhumed from the crypt was strikingly parallel to the account of the reservation of a few of Becket's bones by Archbishop Stephen Langton prior to their translation to the shrine in 1220.

Fifthly, the prominent position of the skull in the coffin, raised up on its stone pillow and surrounded by the other bones, would be consistent with the particular status of Becket's skull as an object of veneration. The blows to his skull that killed him were not only the blows of assassination, they also constituted an act of sacrilegious assault upon the tonsure of a priest. It was this, as well as the fact of murder, that outraged religious opinion in 1170; and his skull (or, at least, something that purported to be his skull) was offered for kissing to generations of pilgrims visiting Canterbury Cathedral in the years after 1220. Moreover, the drawing of Becket's shrine in the Cottonian Manuscripts was, as we have seen, well known for its depiction of an apparently similar arrangement

This Flemish miniature emphasises the sacrilegious nature of Becket's murder: he is kneeling before an altar, with his tonsure and the cross on his chasuble much in evidence; from the Hastings Hours, *c.* 1480.

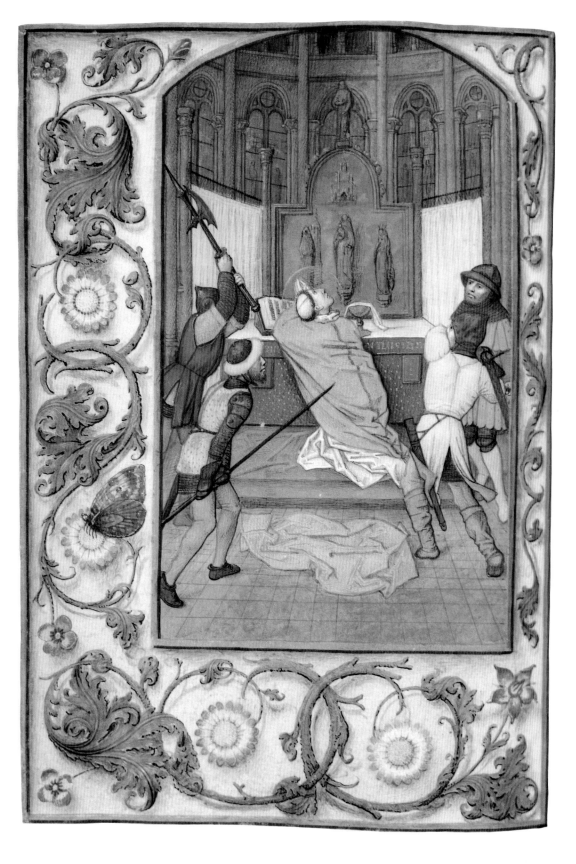

of the bones within the feretrum, with the skull placed in a prominent and central position surrounded by the other bones.

Sixthly, the bones were identified by the surgeon, Mr Thornton, as those of a man aged between about 45 and 55. The age had been confirmed by a dental examination of the few remaining teeth. Becket had probably been born in December 1118, making him about 52 years of age at the time of his martyrdom.

Seventhly, the skeleton was thought by Thornton to have been that of a large man, possibly as tall as six feet two inches. This would have been a distinctive height in the Middle Ages, and it is known from contemporary accounts (including William fitzStephen's biography) that Becket was a tall and strong man. According to a fifteenth-century chronicle he was almost seven feet tall,[6] though it is difficult to reconcile this with the many pictorial representations of his murder, none of which shows him towering distinctively above the knights.[7]

Eighthly, the skull had sustained a number of injuries, most notably a large aperture on the left side that could, in Thornton's opinion, have been caused by a heavy cutting instrument such as a two-handed sword. Although the precise sequence of the knights' attacks on Becket cannot be determined from contemporary documents, it is likely that he received about four blows to the head, at least one of which caused such grievous damage to the skull that Hugh of Horsea was able to draw out the brains and blood through the wound and scatter them on the stone floor.

Lastly, the head and the base of a bishop's or archbishop's effigy, sculpted in high relief in Purbeck marble, was found in the earthen floor surrounding the coffin, possibly indicative of the ecclesiastical office of the deceased man.[8]

Taken together, these findings, many of which became widely known within a short time of the discovery of the coffin, seemed to point strongly towards the likelihood of the bones being those of Becket. News of the find spread very quickly. For reasons that are not clear, the Dean and Chapter must have been in almost immediate contact with the local and national press, informing them not only of the discovery but also of the possible connection with Becket. The *Morning Post* reported on 28 January that 'the theory is put forward that at the time of the burning of the bones of Thomas à Becket in the reign of Henry VIII, three centuries after the murder of the Archbishop, a portion of them may have been secured and buried'.[9] On 2 February the paper reported that 'the result of the investigation up to the present confirms the first impression that the remains are really those of the murdered Primate. This theory is based particularly upon the condition of the skull'.[10] The next day, only eleven days after the discovery, the *Morning Post* went so far as to declare that 'the remains found a few days ago in a rough-hewn coffer in Canterbury Cathedral have practically proved to be those of Thomas à Becket'.[11] In another report on the excavation, *The Times* actually informed its readers that 'the remains of Thomas à Becket have been discovered'.[12]

This view did not, of course, pass unchallenged, and a debate about the identification of the bones began in the correspondence columns of *The Times* on the very day the skeleton was reinterred in its grave in the eastern crypt (10 February 1888). Since positive proof of its identification was never likely, the most that could be advanced or challenged was an hypothesis about its identification as Becket's. The debate was quickly under way between those who advanced the hypothesis (the 'believers'), those who rejected it (the 'sceptics'), and those declared themselves unable or unwilling to express an opinion (the 'agnostics').

Prominent among the 'believers' in the Becket hypothesis was Mr H.G. Austin, the Cathedral surveyor, who had been in charge of the excavations in the crypt in 1888.[13] Austin was among the first to see the coffin and its contents; it was to his house in the precincts that the bones were removed in their cardboard box; it was he who delighted at the visit of the man from Margate and his blind son; and it was he who supervised the reinterment. Austin's enthusiastic espousal of the case for Becket brought him into sharp conflict with others of the Cathedral staff. Miss Holland, in her correspondence with Miss Rawlinson, remarked that he was 'daggers drawn' with Dr Joseph Brigstock Sheppard (the Seneschal of Canterbury and one of the three members of the Investigating Committee), who regarded the idea as 'piff paff' and 'rubbish'.[14] Sheppard further succeeded in enraging Austin by implying that the skull had been damaged in the course of its removal from the coffin.[15]

The grounds of Austin's belief are not entirely clear. According to Miss Holland, he was persuaded by the apparent facts that the bones had been placed in the coffin after they had become a skeleton; that the coffin was the very one in which Becket had originally been buried (though there was no mention of this in the report of the Investigating Committee); and that the place in which it was found was an honoured one.[16] Austin himself contributed to the correspondence in *The Times*, in which he further claimed that the pattern of fractures on the skull was consistent with the contemporary accounts of the knights' assault on Becket.[17]

A second prominent 'believer', though seemingly less passionate than Austin, was Canon Charles Routledge. Routledge, who had by this time been an honorary canon of Canterbury for almost a decade, had been educated at Eton and Cambridge, where he had taken a first in classics. He remained a voracious reader of classical literature throughout his life. In parallel with his career in the Church, he was also one of Her Majesty's Inspectors of Schools, a post he held from 1864 until shortly before his death in 1904.

As a member of the three-man Investigating Committee, Routledge was presumably obliged to subjugate his personal opinion on the identity of the bones to that of the committee as a whole. It is clear, however, that he was sympathetic from the outset to the idea that the skeleton was that of Becket, and his conviction seems to have strengthened with the passage of time. In his own contribution to the correspondence in *The Times*, for example, he pointed to the absence of direct evidence that Becket's remains had been burned when the shrine was dismantled in 1538, and he actually described any such burning as 'very improbable'. 'I myself am strongly of the opinion,' Routledge concluded, 'that the bones found – if not those of St Thomas – are at any rate the relics of some distinguished person, mercifully and reverently placed in the coffin . . . in a place of great traditional sanctity.'[18]

A few years later, in 1895, Routledge wrote again on the subject.[19] Noting the continuing controversy over the identification of the bones, Routledge declared that his purpose was to give a short summary of the issues, and he did this in a way that laid bare his personal sympathies. He first reviewed the now familiar arguments in favour of the Becket hypothesis: the dramatic location of the coffin, the fact that the bones had been placed there as bones and not as a body, the large stature of the man whose skeleton it had been, and the possibility of the wounds to the head having been caused by a heavy cutting instrument. 'There seems therefore so far,' he concluded, 'much plausibility in the idea that the bones found were those of Archbishop Becket.'

Routledge then turned to the counter-arguments, of which he found three principal ones: that the skull was much less damaged than might have been expected from the terrible blows inflicted upon Becket; that Becket's remains had been burned in 1538 and not buried; and that nothing had been done to reinstate the shrine during the Catholic restoration of Mary Tudor's reign. On each of these counter-arguments (which will be examined in greater detail in later chapters), Routledge marshalled sufficient evidence to dismiss them to his own satisfaction. He concluded his article with these words:

> The bones discovered in 1888 are almost certainly the remains of some distinguished saint, and it appears to me quite a probable conjecture that they are the veritable relics of St Thomas of Canterbury. In this

case we trust that at no distant time the Dean and Chapter of Canterbury will see their way to erect over them a memorial befitting their
historical interest.[20]

As will be seen, such a memorial was very nearly erected more than fifty
years later – but not quite.

A third 'believer' who, like Routledge, became increasingly convinced
with the passage of time, was the surgeon who was called in to examine
the bones, Mr W. Pugin Thornton. Thornton qualified as a member of the
Royal College of Surgeons in 1872 and was admitted to the Medical
Register of the General Medical Council in July 1877. He was at that time
living in County Galway, and he died in Ireland in 1913. It is not known
for how long he was living or practising in Canterbury, nor why he
should have been summoned by the Dean and Chapter to examine and
report upon the bones laid out on the white deal boards in Mr Austin's
house in the precincts.

At first, Thornton was cautious in his attribution. In the published
version of his report to the Dean and Chapter he went no farther than
to remark 'if this be Thomas à Becket's skull ...'.[21] Similarly, in his first
contribution to the debate in *The Times*, Thornton used equally guarded
language, describing the bones as *'supposed* to be those of Thomas à
Becket'.[22] A little later, however, his mind seems to have been rather
more firmly made up: in a second letter to *The Times* he declared that the
size of the skull and the computed age of the skeleton's owner 'tend to
prove the association between Thomas à Becket and this skeleton'.[23]
Later still, in a reflective pamphlet first published in 1901 and running
eventually to several editions, Thornton came to the conclusion that 'the
reasons for believing that the bones ... were those of Archbishop Becket
are ample'.[24] Among the reasons he cited were the familiar ones about
the antiquity and size of the skeleton, the age and character of its erstwhile owner, the distinctive location in which it had been placed, and the
fact that the interment had evidently been an act of reburial, not of burial.
Like Routledge, Thornton was also able to satisfy himself that Becket's
remains had probably been buried in 1538, not burned.

So much for the principal 'believers' in the immediate aftermath of
the discovery of the coffin and its contents. One of the self-confessed
'agnostics', at least initially, was Miss Holland, who witnessed much of
the flurry of activity in the crypt and around the precincts. Exposed first
to one opinion and then another, Miss Holland confessed to her correspondent, Miss Rawlinson, that 'I do not know what to think about it all,
and find myself always agreeing with the last person, which is very
weak, of course'.[25] In her next letter she admitted that 'I cannot make up

my mind to anything except that these are the bones of some distinguished and holy man'.[26] Finally, however, she seems to have veered
towards the 'sceptics', declaring in her letter of 1 March 1888 that 'I can
no longer believe that our relics are those of St Thomas of Canterbury'.[27]

Possibly the most important 'agnostic' note was sounded by the
Investigating Committee itself. Commenting on the bones in its published report, the Committee blandly remarked that 'there is no distinct
evidence to shew to whom they belong'.[28] This may perhaps have been a
compromise statement negotiated between Routledge (who instinctively
wanted to believe that the bones were Becket's), Sheppard (who was
quite clear that they were not), and Scott Robertson (whose personal
views on the matter are not known). At all events, the Dean and
Chapter's response to the report was muted in the extreme: the meeting
of the Chapter in May 1888 simply decided 'to receive the reports of
Canons Scott Robertson and Routledge and of Mr Thornton'.[29] At a later
meeting of the Chapter in July 1888, 'the report of the excavations made
in the Cathedral was laid upon the table'.[30] No further references to the
matter are to be found in the *Minutes of the Canterbury Chapter*, and the
Dean does not appear to have taken any further his positive response to
Miss Holland's suggestion that the site of the coffin should be marked in
some way.

Those sceptical about the Becket hypothesis were both local and
national. The most prominent local sceptic was Dr Joseph Brigstock
Sheppard. Although he appears to have left no written statement of
his personal views on the identity of the skeleton, Miss Holland's correspondence reveals him as amusingly, even disdainfully, dismissive of
the idea that it might have been Becket's.[31] The grounds for Sheppard's
scepticism seem to have sprung from the conventional assumption that
the saint's bones had been burned by the King's Commissioners in 1538
and could not therefore have been those taken from the coffin. In this he
was supported by the Precentor of Lincoln Cathedral, the Very Reverend
Edmund Venables, who had written extensively on antiquarian topics
and who was a member of the Royal Archaeological Institute. Venables's
contribution to the debate in *The Times* consisted of a rehearsal of the
testimony of two sixteenth-century chroniclers, Charles Wriothesley and
John Stow, that Becket's bones had indeed been burned in 1538 by the
Lord Privy Seal, Thomas Cromwell, and the ashes scattered to the
winds.[32]

The most consistent and forceful of the contemporary 'sceptics' was a
priest from the Jesuit community in Farm Street, London. In a series of
lengthy and authoritative letters to *The Times* in February and March
1888, Father John Morris repeatedly attacked the hypothesis that these

might be the remains of St Thomas of Canterbury. In this matter, Morris was in no doubt whatsoever.

Father John Morris was an important figure in the Roman Catholic Church in England in the latter years of the nineteenth century. Born in India in 1826, he attended Harrow School and went up to Trinity College, Cambridge in 1845; within a year he had embraced the Catholic faith and was received into the Roman communion in May 1846. His conversion to Rome was said in the *Dictionary of National Biography* to have caused 'some sensation'. There then followed three years of study at the English College in Rome, where he was ordained priest in 1849. Morris remained in Rome as vice-rector of the English College until 1855, when he returned to England to become private secretary first to Cardinal Wiseman and then, in 1861, to his successor, Cardinal Manning.

In 1867 Morris fulfilled his long-cherished goal of entering the Society of Jesus. He took his first vows at Louvain in 1869. Two years later he was appointed Professor of Ecclesiastical History and Canon Law in the College of St Bueno, north Wales. In 1880 he became rector and master of novices at Roehampton, an office that he held for six years, and in 1891 he was appointed head of the staff of the Jesuit writers at Farm Street, in London. Morris retired to Wimbledon in 1893, where he died with 'startling suddenness' the same year while preaching in church on a Sunday morning in October.

Morris took a special interest in the English martyrs, his efforts resulting in the beatification by Pope Leo XIII of More, Fisher, and others. He was a regular contributor to the scholarly Catholic periodical the *Month*. His most important work, published in three volumes between 1872 and 1877, was *The Trouble with our Catholic Forefathers*; but he had earlier written a large and scholarly *Life and Martyrdom of St Thomas Becket, Archbishop of Canterbury*, first published in 1859 and running eventually to several impressions. He was, then, an acknowledged authority on Becket long before the bones made their dramatic appearance in Canterbury Cathedral in January 1888.

Father Morris visited Canterbury to view the bones on at least two occasions before their reinterment,[33] in the course of which he saw the surgeon, Thornton, at work on the skeleton.[34] It seems, however, that Morris may not have exchanged much information with the local experts, as he was quickly in print with his own views about the identification of the bones, only to retract some of his early assertions when corrected by Canon Routledge, Mr Austin and Mr Thornton.

Morris's first letter to *The Times* was published on the very day of the reinterment.[35] In it, he set out the first of the two major arguments against the Becket hypothesis: that the injuries to the skull were inconsistent with

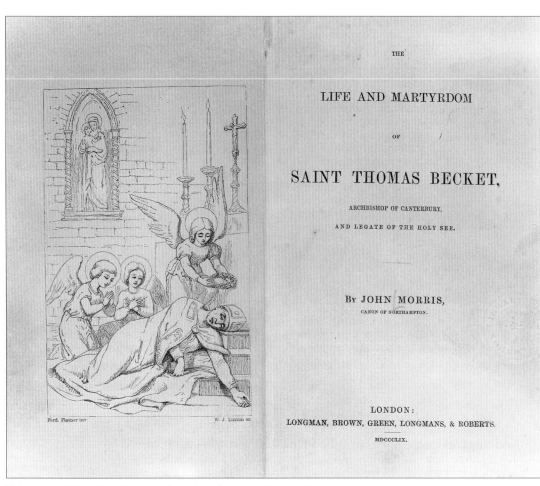

Titlepage of *The Life and Martyrdom of St Thomas Becket* by John Morris, 1859.

the contemporary accounts of the sword blows sustained by the Archbishop at his martyrdom. Morris drew the clear conclusion from these accounts that the blows were such as to sever totally the crown of Becket's head: 'corona capitis tota ei amputata est,' as William fitzStephen had put it. That being the case, Morris argued, the skull in question could not have been that of Becket, for its crown was quite uninjured. Not only that, the damage which had obviously been inflicted on the left side of the skull had, Morris believed, been caused not by a sharp cutting instrument such as a sword, but by a blunter instrument such as 'a mace, hammer or quite lately by a digger's pickaxe'.

Morris concluded in this opening letter that the bones had probably belonged to an erstwhile monk of Christ Church Priory who had been

54

reburied in the crypt, along with several others, when the monks' cemetery outside the Cathedral had been disturbed during some building operation. The curious positioning of the bones in the coffin, Morris thought, was simply the result of the coffin having been tilted upwards at the time of its insertion into the grave, causing the loose bones to gather at one end, as they were found.

In his next letters following rejoinders from Austin, Routledge and Thornton,[36] Morris adjusted his position, conceding that the bones were unlikely to have been those of a monk since they had been placed in the coffin as a set of bones, not as a body. He also waived his theory about the coffin having been tilted at the time of its interment, causing the particular gathering of the bones within it. He remained adamant, however, that although 'the bones are probably those of a distinguished person, perhaps an unshrined saint', they could not be Becket's, since the damage to the skull could not possibly be reconciled with the eyewitness accounts of the manner of Becket's death. Becket received at least four blows to his head from the assailant knights, one of which sliced off a section of the crown. Having consulted the curator of the museum of the Royal College of Surgeons, Morris maintained that not only was the crown of the skull found in the crypt intact, the damage in the area of the left temple could not have been caused by a cutting instrument.

Morris then turned to the second major argument against the Becket hypothesis: that the saint's bones had been burned in 1538. He reviewed the evidence in favour of burial rather than burning, and found it wanting. Indeed, Morris claimed that much of the confusion over whether or not the saint's remains had been buried resulted from a spectacular mistranscription of a widely quoted passage from Nicholas Harpsfield's book, *The Life and Death of Sr Thomas More*, the earliest version of which appeared in 1554 and which remained in manuscript form until its publication for the first time in 1932.[37] The passage, comparing the martyrdom of More with that of Becket, purportedly claimed that, on being removed from the shrine in 1538, Becket's remains had indeed been buried. Harpsfield, who had once been a professor of Greek at Oxford, was Archdeacon of Canterbury during the brief period of the Catholic restoration under Mary Tudor, and might therefore be expected to have known precisely what had happened to the bones. For him to be interpreted as saying that they were buried, not burned, struck many antiquarians as a statement of great weight and authority. However, unlike other commentators who had not bothered to check the wording in any of the manuscripts (including the eminently respected Dean Stanley),[38] Morris had looked at one of Harpsfield's original scripts in the British Museum for himself, and found that, far from stating that the bones had been buried, Harpsfield had actually said that they were 'burned'. Of that Morris was in no doubt.

> I not only saw the word 'burned' myself, but two friends of mine also. To make assurance doubly sure, I have been to Lambeth [Palace] to consult the two other manuscripts [of Harpsfield], and I find, as at the British Museum, that ... Harpsfield says 'burned'.[39]

In his final contribution to the correspondence in *The Times* Morris returned to the condition of the skull, attacking the partiality of Thornton's observations about its condition.[40] He had earlier been taken to task yet again by Thornton for allegedly misinterpreting the nature and extent of the damage to the left side of the skull,[41] and again he struck back. 'Why,' Morris asked, 'should Mr Thornton speak of the left side only, and has not a word to say about the right?' The answer, Morris suggested, was that Thornton only saw what he wished to see: it was widely assumed from the contemporary accounts of Becket's slaying that the worst of the knights' blows had fallen only on the left side of the head, and Thornton was (Morris suggested) looking only to see what might confirm the skull as Becket's. But what about the right side? 'On that side', wrote Morris,

> there are, I think, four loose pieces and a couple of small apertures. Why, Sir, what with the crack across the crown, due to the pickaxe, and the opening of the sutures, and other fractures innumerable, I should like to know from Mr Thornton in how many pieces he found the skull when he put it together on this clay mould?

Morris then turned again to the key question of the crown of the skull. Becket, he reiterated, had effectively suffered a total amputation of the crown of his head. Of that there could be no doubt. Even if the accounts of the actual killing were rather inconsistent for reasons of darkness, confusion and panic, the head was seen by the monks the next day in ample time and full daylight. 'There is also,' Morris pointed out, 'the undoubted fact that for two or three centuries the part of the skull that had been cut off was kept separate from the rest, and the two parts were visited and seen by innumerable multitudes.' (In fact, as will be seen in Chapter 7, Morris was probably in error in this assertion.) Morris remarked with impeccable syntax that

> even if we were ignorant of the manner of Becket's death, and if all we knew was that the crown of his head was kept apart from the

perforated skull, we should at once say that a head, however fractured, was not his, the occipital bone of which is in firm articulation with both parietals.

Father Morris finally recapitulated the evidence that Becket's bones had been burned in 1538, and concluded rather tartly that 'I could tell blindfolded that the bones before us are not those of a man whose bones were burned'.

And there for the time being, indecisively, the matter rested.

Woodcut showing Becket's martyrdom
from an indulgence printed in 1515.

4   Debating the Bones

The exchange of views in *The Times* in February and March 1888 about the identification of the bones in the eastern crypt not only failed to answer the question, 'Whose bones are they?', it also failed conclusively to refute the hypothesis that they were the bones of St Thomas Becket. Father Morris's arguments against the hypothesis, first set out in his letters to *The Times* and later published as a pamphlet entitled *The Relics of St Thomas*,[1] were forceful and persuasive: the remains of Becket had been burned in 1538 and the ashes scattered to the winds. Not only that, the damage to the skull was incompatible with the injuries inflicted by the four knights upon Becket's head. Yet, far from fading, the debate moved persistently on, surfacing from time to time in assorted publications.

In the *Standard* a short time after the discovery of the bones, an article on Canterbury Cathedral stated that 'our protestant primates have not hitherto been buried in the Cathedral that holds the remains of Becket'.[2] In a swift rejoinder, a correspondent signing himself simply 'Arkasden' suggested that a slip of the pen had occurred: the passage ought to have read: 'the Cathedral that *held* the remains of Becket'. Like Morris, Arkasden advanced the evidence of the sixteenth-century chroniclers, Wriothesley and Stow, in support of his contention that Becket's bones had been burned in 1538, and concluded: 'Some few years ago a skeleton was found in a stone coffin . . . Nothing of any real value was brought forward which upset the received story that the bones were burned.'

The issue received its next public outing in 1891 when the director of the Society of Antiquaries, Mr Henry Salusbury Milman, read a two-part paper to the society in February and March of that year entitled 'The Vanished Memorials of St Thomas of Canterbury'. It was published the following year as a paper in the journal *Archaeologia*.[3] Milman's paper was a detailed, scholarly and dispassionate account of the once-celebrated memorials of Becket that had been expunged from Canterbury Cathedral at the time of the Reformation. Indeed, so concerned was he to establish the scholarly credentials of the piece that he began his narrative by complaining about 'the confused manner in which the notices of them [had been] treated, the neglect to seek for definite meanings of terms, and the clinging to sham tradition as if it were real history'.[4] Milman claimed that his own paper would remedy the deficit.

Much of the evidence and argument marshalled by Milman is examined in greater detail in Chapter 7. For present purposes, his broad analysis and conclusion concerning the fate of Becket's remains will suffice. It was Milman's contention that the story of the burning of the bones, which, he claimed, first appeared in a papal bull of excommunication against King Henry VIII in December 1538, was 'a misapplication of Roman ideas to England which suggested to the Pope the special wording of his sentence'.[5] Nevertheless, as the story gained credence on the continent, so the King's difficulties increased at home, to the point where he was obliged to issue a public explanation of his policy on the treatment of shrines and relics. The explanation took the form of a statement, written in the hand of the Clerk of the Privy Council, Thomas Derby, that may have been intended as a draft sermon to be preached to the public at St Paul's Cross. Dated 1539, it first set out the general policy on the shrines and reliquaries of saints, and then dealt specifically with the situation at Canterbury. The critical passage, Milman contended, read in the original version that he had consulted as follows:

> As for the shryne of Thomas Becket, sometime Archbishop of Canterbury . . . it was arrested that his shrynes and bones shuld be taken away and bestowed in suche place as the same shuld cause no superstition afterwards, as it is indede amongst others of that sorte conveyed and buried in a noble toure [tower].[6]

The King's purpose in doing this, Milman argued, was to counter the papal propaganda about the burning of Becket's remains. The essential veracity of the 1539 statement was subsequently confirmed in 1552 in a narrative (*Il Pellegrino Inglese*) attributed to William Thomas, 'a man of ability and learning who had been then lately in the suite of the King's ambassador at Venice'. In the narrative Thomas, having related how King Henry VIII had examined the miracles attributed to St Thomas, continued, in the version consulted by Milman:

> The kynge could do no lesse then deface the shryne that was an authour of so muche ydolatry. Whether the doyng thereof hath been the undoyng of the canonised saint or not, I cannot tell. Butt this is true, that his bones are spred amongest the bones of so many dead men, that without some great miracle they will not be found agayne.[7]

Milman was confident, on the basis of this testimony, that Becket's bones had been buried, not burned, in 1538; nevertheless he did not subscribe to the view that the bones taken from the coffin in the crypt in 1888 were the right ones. It was his contention, following Thomas Derby's reference to a 'noble toure', that Becket's remains had actually been buried in the so-called 'corona' at the extreme eastern end of the Trinity Chapel in Canterbury Cathedral. The corona, an unusual feature of English cathedral architecture, is an uncompleted but almost free-standing tower, topped with battlements, which may reasonably be regarded as the tower of the Trinity Chapel. There, together with Becket's bones, went also those of the other unshrined saints of Canterbury, thereby, Milman suggested, satisfying William Thomas's observation about the remains being 'spred amongst the bones of so many dead men'.

Milman's reason for the choice of the corona as Becket's final resting place may appear to be rather insubstantial, for there are several other places in the Cathedral that could just as well be described as a 'noble tower'. By way of further corroboration, however, Milman noted that Cardinal Reginald Pole, the last Roman Catholic Archbishop of Canterbury, was also buried in the corona on 15 December 1558, in accordance with a direction in his will that his body should be placed 'in my church of Canterbury in that chapel in which the head of the most blessed Martyr Thomas, formerly Archbishop of the said church, was kept'. Why, Milman asked, did Pole choose the place where the supposed *head* of Becket had been kept in preference to the crypt, where his entire *body* had originally been buried? Could it not be, he wondered, that Pole 'may have known the secret of the second burial, and ... thus provided, without revealing that secret, that his own bones should rest near those of his holy predecessor'?[8]

Milman's only reference to the bones discovered in 1888 was in the context of establishing that, whoever's bones they may have been, they had certainly not been those of Becket. Nevertheless, Milman acknowledged the many remarkable features of these bones that pointed towards the saint, including the injuries to the skull, the large height of the skeleton, and its conformity with the contemporary accounts of the destruction of the shrine in 1538.

The next contribution to the debate came four years later in 1895 when Canon Charles Routledge, a member of the original Investigating Committee and one of the 'believers' in the Becket hypothesis, published a short article in which he sought to set out a summary of the controversy about the bones.[9] It was, he noted, a controversy that had continued unabated over the previous seven years since the initial discovery of the remains. Routledge first rehearsed the principal arguments in favour of

Canterbury Cathedral: exterior view of the corona at the extreme eastern end of the cathedral.

the bones being those of Becket. They were, briefly: the distinctive site at which the coffin had been found, adjacent to that of Becket's erstwhile tomb; the unusual features of the coffin, suggesting that the interment of the bones had been an act of haste and secrecy; the curious placement of the bones at one end of it; the height and age of the man whose bones they had been; and the damage to the left side of the skull, where Becket was said to have sustained the greatest wounds from the knights' swords.

Turning to the counter-arguments, Routledge first dismissed the intact crown of the skull as irrelevant, arguing that, in the contemporary accounts of Becket's killing, the 'corona' that had supposedly been amputated was not to be taken as the 'crown' of the head in the normal anatomical sense, but rather in its medieval meaning as the tonsure of a priest, 'clipped bare in the middle and retaining a rim of short hair on its edge'.[10] Much would have been made of this corona in the hagiography of Becket, since its amputation would have been seen in the medieval mind as an act of sacrilegious assault on a consecrated area. Routledge satisfied himself on these grounds that the condition of the skull uncovered in the crypt could be consistent with the accounts of Becket's killing: there was no necessary conflict between the removal by sword-cut of the 'corona' in its medieval sense and the intact nature of the crown of the excavated skull.

Routledge then dismissed the other major counter-argument: that Becket's remains had been burned in 1538. He accepted the force of the evidence of the chroniclers, Wriothesley and Stow, about the burning, but cited two further sources suggesting that the bones had actually been buried. One was Nicholas Harpsfield's *The Life and Death of Sr Thomas More*, although in citing this Routledge made no attempt to address the fatal flaw to which Father Morris had earlier drawn attention, namely that, though much misquoted to the contrary, Harpsfield had actually written that the bones had been burned, not buried.[11] The second source was the paper, described above, that had been read by Milman to the Society of Antiquaries in 1891. Routledge enthusiastically quoted Milman's evidence that Becket's bones had been 'buried in a noble toure' and that they had been 'spred amongst the bones of so many dead men that without some greate miracle they will not be found agayne'.

Routledge thought it plausible that Becket's bones had been taken secretly by the monks from the shrine in the Trinity Chapel, either before its destruction or subsequently with the approval of the King's Commissioners, and deposited in the place in the crypt, adjacent to the site of his original tomb, in which the coffin had been discovered in 1888. He thought it a 'quite probable conjecture' that they were the veritable

The Trinity Chapel looking east across the site of
Becket's shrine towards the corona beyond.

relics of the saint, and he hoped that a suitable memorial would be erected over the place.

In 1901 the surgeon who had originally examined the skeleton, Mr W. Pugin Thornton, kept the pot boiling by publishing his little reflective pamphlet, *Becket's Bones*.[12] It has already been observed (Chapter 3) that Thornton had by this time become a staunch 'believer' in the Becket hypothesis; and while it is unclear why he felt it necessary to go into print again on the matter, his pamphlet left its readers in no doubt about his views. Interestingly, Thornton placed little reliance at this stage on the state of the skull, though it was he who had first excited comment through his observation that the great wound on the left side may have been caused by a sharp cutting instrument such as a two-handed sword.[13] He may perhaps by this time have been entertaining doubts about the accuracy of his original observations. For whatever reason, by 1901 Thornton was much more impressed by the special location of the coffin, the positioning of the bones within it, and the unusually large size of the man whose skeleton it had been. These considerations amounted in his view to 'ample reasons' for believing the bones to be those of Becket.

The Society of Antiquaries was again the setting for the next act in the drama, when the honorary librarian to the Dean and Chapter of Canterbury, Mr M. Beazeley, FRGS, read a paper in December 1907, 'On Certain Human Remains Found in the Crypt of Canterbury Cathedral and Supposed by Some to be Those of Archbishop Becket'. The text of Beazeley's paper was published in the *Proceedings of the Society of Antiquaries*,[14] and was also summarised four days later in *The Times*. The substance of it, with some later amendments, was later published as *The Canterbury Bones*.[15] This pamphlet is not dated, but from its context it must have been published in 1913 or 1914, probably the former date.

In his paper, Beazeley categorised the issue into three questions, the first two of which must by this time have been very familiar to his audience: is there evidence to show that the remains found in 1888 were actually those of Becket, and were Becket's bones really burned at the time of the destruction of the shrine in 1538? The third question, however, was novel:

> Supposing it to be ascertained that the remains in question were *not* Becket's, what evidence is there to show whose they were?[16]

On the first question, Beazeley had no difficulty in aligning himself with Milman and Arkasden against Routledge and Thornton: the bones, in his view, were emphatically not Becket's. Some, though not all, of his reasons were new. He thought, for example, that the skeleton, which had been measured by Thornton to be as much as six feet and two inches in height, was actually too short to be Becket's. Beazeley maintained that the saint had, according to a fifteenth-century chronicle, been only an inch short of seven feet in life.[17] Beazeley noted that the skull, when found, had only five teeth remaining, a number which he took to be far fewer than would be expected of a man of Becket's age and supposedly vigorous health. Beazeley was also quite unimpressed by the store that Thornton had set on the circumference of the skull (22.75 inches) as indicative of a man of extraordinary vitality and intelligence. 'This size of head,' Beazeley maintained, 'is by no means anything at all unusual among the cultured classes of this country, only representing, as it does, a size in hats of $7^{1}/_{8}$.'[18] By way of empirical amplification, Beazeley quoted the list of hat sizes supplied by Messrs Lincoln and Bennett, 27 per cent of which equalled this size and 25 per cent of which exceeded it.

The remaining reasons given by Beazeley for rejecting the Becket hypothesis were by now quite standard, most obviously that the injuries to the skull bore no resemblance to those that must have been inflicted on the Archbishop's head by the swords of his assailants. He returned to novel ground, however, in addressing his second question: whether Becket's remains had been burned at the time of the destruction of the shrine. On this point, Beazeley disagreed with Milman (whose view had been that, far from being burned, they had actually been buried in the corona at the eastern end of the Trinity Chapel). Beazeley was in no doubt about the burning, partly because of the familiar evidence of Harpsfield, Wriothesley and Stow, but also because of what he described as 'startling' new evidence that had recently been uncovered by another Jesuit priest, Father J.H. Pollen. Like Father John Morris twenty years earlier, Pollen was an eminent and well-respected Catholic historian; and, also like Morris, he too had a special interest in the English martyrs. He was a prolific contributor to the scholarly Catholic periodical the *Month*, writing often about the Catholic dimension of the Reformation.

In an article published in the *Month* in 1908,[19] Pollen had reported on a hitherto unnoticed entry in the *Calendar of State Papers* to the effect that not only had the Lord Privy Seal, Thomas Cromwell, been present at the destruction of the shrine in September 1538, but that the King himself had also been in Canterbury at the time. The document in question was a letter from John Hussee, a servant of Lord Lisle, to Lady Lisle. Dated 8 September 1538, it said that 'my Lord is so entertained, especially with the King and my Lord Privy Seal, that he is not like to depart till the King has removed from Canterbury ...'. This new evidence was, for Beazeley, a hugely important factor. For if the remains had been secretly removed and buried by the monks before the arrival of the Commissioners, as

Milman and others had hypothesised, then either the shrine was empty when it was opened by the Commissioners or it contained substitute bones. 'It matters not which,' Beazeley remarked,

> as either supposition is too incredible to be entertained . . . . [The monks] would not have dared to commit such an act, knowing full well what the result of it to themselves would be. For had they done so, with the King, Cromwell, Windsor Herald and the Commissioners directing affairs, there must have been many present who would have handed up those concerned in the fraud, who would have had short shrift indeed, as in Tudor days swift and severe punishment was awarded for serious offences. Yet there is no record of any such punishment having been meted out.[20]

(In passing, it may be noted that Beazeley was in error in stating that the Windsor Herald was present at the opening of the shrine. The implications of this rather serious error are discussed in Chapter 7.)

In turning to his third question – whose skeleton was it if not Becket's? – Beazeley embarked on truly innovative ground. It was, he proposed, the skeleton of William de Audeville. The idea was not, strictly, Beazeley's own: it had been suggested to him by the late Mr William Pugh, a former vesturer of the Cathedral, who had actually been present at the opening of the coffin in 1888. It was, however, an idea that obviously commended itself to Beazeley. At the time of his death in January 1159, de Audeville was Abbot of the great Benedictine monastery of Evesham in Worcestershire, but he was an erstwhile monk of Christ Church Priory who died in Canterbury while attending an archiepiscopal visitation. Beazeley thought that the place of the Abbot's burial in the Cathedral was unambiguously indicated in an extract from the *Chronicles of the Abbots of Evesham*, published in the Rolls Series.

> To him [Abbot William] succeeded William de Audeville, a monk of Christ Church, Canterbury, where he lies buried at the head of the blessed Thomas the Martyr, who before he went there by reason of a visitation, when he was visited there by the Lord [ie he died], saw in dreams, as he reported to the brethren, that the sun had been buried at his feet. Which vision received its interpretation in process of time, after the blessed Thomas was buried at his feet.[21]

Of course, de Audeville died some twelve years before Becket, when the site in the crypt had no special significance. There is therefore nothing intrinsically inappropriate about the Abbot's burial there: it was only later, after Becket's body had rested in the adjacent bay for fifty years (i.e., at de Audeville's feet) that the place became distinctive. Nevertheless, there are obvious grounds for rejecting Beazeley's ingenious claim about the ownership of the bones. These are examined in detail in Chapter 8.

A lively discussion followed Beazeley's presentation of his paper to the Society of Antiquaries,[22] reflecting the divided opinion that existed. Mr C. Trice Martin thought that the evidence for the burning of Becket's remains was insubstantial, and that it was an accusation concocted by foreigners. (This, essentially, had been Milman's argument to the society sixteen years earlier.) Mr Aymer Vallance regarded the whole issue of the burning as irrelevant: he had actually seen the bones in 1888 and was convinced they were not those of Becket. Dr Hamilton Hall felt that the condition of the skull was immaterial, since it would be quite impossible to take the crown of a man's head off with a sword-cut. Mr W. St John Hope saw no incompatibility between the 1888 skull and that of a man who had been murdered in the precise way in which Becket had been. The Reverend R.B. Gardiner, Mr J.G. Wood and Mr A.F. Leach also spoke, but their contributions are not recorded.

An equivocal view on the issue was expressed in 1912 by two of the most thorough and respected historians of Canterbury Cathedral, the Reverend C. Eveleigh Woodruff (librarian to the Dean and Chapter) and Canon William Danks (Canon Residentiary). In their exhaustive account of the history of the Cathedral, Woodruff and Danks noted the discovery in recent years of

> a rude stone sarcophagus under the pavement of the crypt, containing the bones of a tall man with a cleft skull, and it has been argued that . . . the remains of Becket were hidden and removed by the monks, who substituted others to undergo the sacrilegious violence of the King.[23]

In summarising the debate in this way, Woodruff and Danks managed to bring together the hypotheses of burial and of burning in a single framework. Becket's bones had been buried and substitute ones had been burned. But they then proceeded to reject the idea that a substitute body had been burned:

> Until this conjecture is supported by further evidence we prefer to accept the statement that the saint's bones were burnt or obscurely buried.[24]

It seems clear from this that Woodruff and Danks were of an open mind about the fate of Becket's remains, and therefore also about the identity

Dante's tomb at the church of
the Frati Minori, Ravenna.

of the tall man with a cleft skull. Many years later, however, Woodruff seemed to have decided against the Becket hypothesis: writing about the cult of St Thomas, he thought that, had the bones in fact been his, it was inconceivable that they would not have been restored to a more honourable resting place during the Catholic revival under Mary Tudor.[25]

The next major contribution to the controversy not only appeared in a somewhat unexpected place, but also introduced dramatic new material. It came in 1917 in the fourth of a series of *Studies in Dante*, subtitled *Textual Criticism of the Convivio and Miscellaneous Essays*, and it concerned the tomb of the Italian medieval poet, Dante Alighieri.[26] Its author, Dr Edward Moore, was another of the several scholarly Victorian and Edwardian clergymen whose enquiring minds were attracted to the skeleton in the eastern crypt. Moore was born in 1835, the elder son of a

Welsh doctor, and took a first in classics and mathematics at Pembroke College, Oxford. He was ordained in 1861 (the year in which Father John Morris became private secretary to Cardinal Manning) and three years later was appointed by Queen's College, Oxford to the principalship of St Edmund Hall. During the fifty years in which he held the post, Moore established the reputation of St Edmund Hall as a home of 'true religion and sound learning' (*Dictionary of National Biography*), increasing its numbers and ensuring its representation in almost every honours list in the University. He was nominated to a canonry at Canterbury in 1903, where for a brief period he shared the canons' stalls with Charles Routledge.

Moore spent much of his later time as principal of St Edmund Hall fighting the University's proposals to end the separate existence of the Hall by merging it with Queen's College. His success in ensuring the independent continuation of St Edmund enabled the Hall to be associated with two other men who enter the story in Chapter 6: John Shirley, who studied there under Moore between 1909 and 1912 and himself became a canon of Canterbury, and Mr Alfred Emden, who was principal from 1929 to 1951 and later a close friend of Shirley. Moore eventually retired to Canterbury in 1913, where he was an active member of the Chapter. He died in 1916, before the publication of his fourth series of *Studies in Dante*. In his memory, his friends restored the Jesus Chapel in the eastern crypt at Canterbury – just a few yards east of the grave discovered in 1888.

Moore achieved international recognition as an authority on Dante. In 1876 he founded the Oxford Dante Society, and ten years later was appointed Barlow Lecturer on Dante at University College, London. In 1895 a Dante lectureship was specially created for him at the Taylorian Institute at Oxford. His most important work, published in 1889, was *Contributions to the Textual Criticism of the Divina Commedia*, an epic piece of scholarship that placed him in the forefront of living Dante scholars. Later came the *Oxford Dante* (1894) and the four series of *Studies in Dante*. Among the many honours he received was the Fellowship of the British Academy in 1906.

Dante Alighieri was born in Florence in 1265 and died in Ravenna on 14 September 1321. When he was buried in the Franciscan church of the Frati Minori, adjoining the monastery at Ravenna, his body was clothed in the vestments of the Franciscan order in which he is said to have expressed a wish to die. His body was deposited in a stone sarcophagus which, though the object was actually frustrated, was intended to have been a temporary resting place until a more fitting sepulchre could be constructed. From the outset, Dante's body, like that of Becket, was

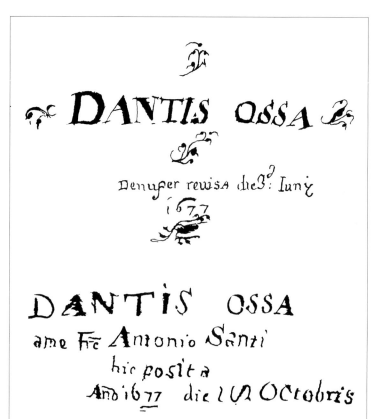

The two inscriptions found on the chest containing the bones read: 'Dante's bones, revisited anew 3 June 1677' and 'Dante's bones placed here by Fra Antonio Santi October, 1677'.

under physical threat from those who had, in life, been his enemies: in 1322, only a year after his death, Cardinal Bertrand de Poyet, the papal legate, threatened to open the tomb, burn the bones, and scatter the ashes.

On 27 May 1865, twenty-three years before the discovery of the coffin at Canterbury, workmen were engaged in removing a portion of wall in an outlying chapel of the church of the Frati Minori, a short distance away from Dante's tomb. While removing some bricks that had been used to block up an old doorway, they uncovered an ancient wooden chest. It fell to pieces, disclosing some human bones and words (in Latin) written on the floor: 'The bones of Dante, revisited anew, June 3rd 1677'. A similar inscription was discovered on one of the outer planks of the chest. The skeleton was found to be complete, with the exception of a few small bones.

Attention then obviously turned to Dante's tomb, in which it had naturally been assumed that his remains had lain since 1321, and the tomb was opened on 7 June 1865. It was found to be empty, save for a few bones which corresponded to those missing from the chest and some broken fragments of the same marble as the tomb itself. Further examination revealed that a rough hole had been knocked through the back of the tomb, in a place that could have been accessible only from the monastery itself. There could be no doubt that Dante's bones had been removed through this aperture, nor that the newly discovered bones were indeed those of the poet. It was impossible to say how long the bones might have been kept hidden in the monastery between their removal from the tomb and their final immurement in the wooden chest in 1677, but Moore suggested that it might have been for several generations.

The reason for this extraordinary treatment of one of Renaissance Italy's greatest treasures can only be guessed at. A possible explanation may have been the fear of the monks that their supreme possession might be snatched away from them in favour of a more distinguished resting place. The people of Florence, for example, had actually made four such threats, most formidably in 1519 – the date at which Moore thought the remains had first been removed from the tomb. If so, the dreadful secret had been kept within the monastic community for over 150 years – a remarkable illustration not only of the willingness of a community of monks in the sixteenth century to remove and hide the mortal remains of a great person when they were threatened, but also of their capacity to maintain and transmit the secret from one generation to another over a long period of time.

The episode of Dante's tomb occurred, of course, in Italy; yet Moore proceeded to discuss a somewhat similar case that took place in England, that of St Cuthbert at Durham. The essence of the story is told in Sir Walter Scott's allusion to Cuthbert in his poem *Marmion*:

> There deep in Durham's Gothic shade
> His relics are in secret laid,
> But none may know the place
> Save of his holiest servants three
> Who share that wondrous grace.[27]

Moore drew for his material upon *The Victoria History of the County of Durham*, published in 1905.[28] Cuthbert, the great northern saint, died at Lindisfarne in 687. Eleven years later his body was transferred from its original stone casket to a new wooden coffin which was eventually, in 998, brought to Durham. There it remained buried, with the exception of the years 1069–70 when it was taken back to Lindisfarne in fear of the threatened approach of William the Conqueror. As with Becket at

Canterbury, Cuthbert's shrine became deeply associated with miracles of healing, contributing handsomely to the wealth of the Benedictine monastery at Durham.

In 1537, a year earlier than at Canterbury, Henry VIII's Commissioners arrived in Durham to destroy the shrine of Cuthbert. The coffin containing his remains was forced open with such violence that one of the leg bones was broken.[29] The coffin and its contents were then left in the Cathedral revestry to await the King's decision on their disposal. The monks, fearful of what might happen to the saint's relics, are said by Benedictine tradition to have removed them from the coffin and buried them in another part of the Cathedral, near the west end. The tradition further states that the bones of another monk were taken from the monks' cemetery outside the Cathedral and substituted in the coffin for those of Cuthbert.

Moore believed that, at the time he was writing (1915–16), this tradition was still current in the Benedictine community. At this point, however, the tradition appears to divide, reaching two mutually inconsistent conclusions. One, which seems to have been in circulation until about the end of the nineteenth century, held that the saint's bones remained buried in the Cathedral, in a place known only to three Benedictine monks in each generation (the 'holiest servants three', in Scott's poem). In 1867 two documents from the seventeenth and eighteenth centuries came to light, describing in somewhat vague terms the location of the burial place, and excavations were carried out by the Dean and Chapter. Nothing was found, and the Benedictines reportedly told the Dean and Chapter that they had searched in the wrong place. The reactions of the Dean and Chapter are not recorded!

The alternative conclusion held that, once the danger from the King's Commissioners had passed, the bones of the substitute monk were removed from the coffin, and those of Cuthbert were reinstated before the coffin was reburied behind the high altar in 1542. That this is the more likely explanation first became apparent in 1827 when the coffin was opened and all the signs pointed towards the bones therein being genuinely those of Cuthbert. There was no indication that they had ever been exposed to the damp conditions that undoubtedly existed in the monks' cemetery; a thigh bone, presumed to be that which had been rudely broken by the Commissioners in 1537, was missing; and a number of religious artefacts which were known to have been in the coffin when it was examined in 1104 were still hidden within the coverings in which the body was wrapped.

The matter seems to have been finally resolved in 1899 when the coffin was opened yet again, and further tests showed such a measure of agreement between the contents and condition of the coffin and what was indisputably known about Cuthbert's life and death, that there could be no further room for doubt. There now seems to be widespread acceptance that the tomb in Durham Cathedral which today bears his name also contains his true remains.

There are some obvious parallels between the stories of Dante and Cuthbert, though the former is much more substantial. It is beyond dispute that Dante's bones were removed from the tomb in Ravenna; there is no more than a persistent tradition that a similar removal took place in Durham. Nevertheless, Moore was plainly impressed by the similarities between the two stories, adding to them (though failing to give his sources) the third case of St Chad at Lichfield. There, the saint's bones were hurriedly removed from their shrine by one of the prebendaries in about 1537 when the threat of a visitation by the King's Commissioners began to loom.

Encouraged by these similarities, Moore turned his attention to the Canterbury bones. Unsurprisingly, he saw in them a fourth case to parallel the other three.

Moore first noted that the monks of Christ Church Priory had had three clear months' notice in 1538 of what might befall their community. 'It is hardly conceivable,' he argued, 'that some of them should not have profited from this interval to remove the saint's bones and substitute others in their place.'[30] It would, of course, have been an enterprise of great danger and difficulty, but it could have been accomplished by carrying the bones down one of the staircases leading from the Trinity Chapel to the crypt beneath. Once there, nothing could be more understandable than that the monks should choose to inter them in a place 'pointed out by pious sentiment as being that of Becket's original grave, as well as by its convenient proximity to the shrine'.[31]

Nor would this have been the first occasion on which Becket's bones had been removed for their own safety: as in the legend of Cuthbert at Durham, so Becket's remains at Canterbury had been taken from their marble tomb in the crypt shortly after their first burial in 1170 and hidden for safe keeping in a wooden chest behind the altar of Our Lady in the Undercroft (see Chapter 1).

Moore then referred to the proposition, advanced a few years earlier by Beazeley,[32] that the bones in the crypt were actually those of the Abbot of Evesham, William de Audeville. This, Moore argued, was simply not credible: the Abbot could not possibly have been buried in a coffin much too small for his body, without any shroud or garments, only three inches below the surface. In any case, there was no known reason why the Abbot should have sustained a large fracture to his skull. It was much

more probable, Moore argued, that the monks, having encountered de Audeville's coffin while excavating the ground for the reinterment of Becket's bones, removed the Abbot's bones from it and deposited them in Becket's shrine in the Trinity Chapel for the Commissioners to find and burn!

An obvious attraction of this argument was its ability to explain away the supposed burning of Becket's remains by the Commissioners: bones were indeed taken from the shrine and burned, but they happened to be those of the Abbot, not the Archbishop. After all, Moore pointed out, none of the contemporary accounts actually stated that it was the bones of Becket that were burned, merely those that were taken from the shrine. It can be no more than an assumption that the bones were Becket's.

Having thus neatly disposed of one of the principal objections consistently raised against the Becket hypothesis – that his remains had been burned in 1538 – Moore turned his attention to two others. The objection that the wounds to the skull were inconsistent with the knights' assault on Becket (especially the apparent absence of any damage to the crown of the skull) was met with two rejoinders. First, Moore pointed out that the contemporary accounts of Becket's martyrdom were inconsistent and conflicting. There was no single or agreed version of the slaying with which the skull was obliged to be consistent: 'After reading these strangely conflicting narratives, one is almost tempted to adopt the cynical dictum of Lord Palmerston that there is nothing more deceptive than figures except facts'.[33]

Secondly, Moore echoed the point made several years earlier by Routledge,[34] that the crown of Becket's head, which was generally agreed to have been in some sense severed or amputated in the attack, must be understood in its medieval meaning of the priestly tonsure consecrated to God by holy unction, not as a section of bone at the back or top of the head. Indeed, Moore thought it doubtful whether a sword blow could have severed or sliced off the cap of the skull itself. A priest's tonsure was a sacred site, and Moore argued that it was natural that any such sacrilegious assault on the Archbishop should be specially emphasised in the stories that were circulated about his martyrdom. Such stories might well have been fuelled by a dream that Becket himself supposedly had in exile in Pontigny in 1166, in which he had seen himself in a church, pleading his cause before the Pope, when four knights came in, dragged him forth, and slew him by cutting off the crown of his head where he was tonsured.[35]

The second principal objection addressed by Moore was that of the failure to reinstate Becket's bones, if they really had been buried in the

Chapel of Our Lady in the Undercroft.

crypt, during the reign of Mary Tudor. Surely, it had been urged, someone would have

> come forward and earned immense glory, and no doubt very substantial rewards, by proclaiming a secret which would have been hailed throughout the country, and even in the Roman Church at large, as revealing a providential and even miraculous preservation of the most precious relics?[36]

To this Moore replied that, in the fifteen-year interval between the destruction of the shrine and Mary's ascent to the throne, the few monks who had been privy to the dreadful secret would have scattered, died, or had their mouths sealed. 'What could be more natural,' Moore asked rhetorically, 'than that the secret should have entirely perished in those fifteen years, while the persistently repeated story of the public burning of the (supposed) bones of Becket would exclude any suspicion that the question could ever be reopened?'[37]

The process of forgetting would, Moore suggested, have been further encouraged by the walling off of the eastern crypt in 1546, which would have removed the site from public consciousness. Conversely, the process of remembering would have been discouraged by the fact that, with the apparently sole exception of Edward the Confessor at Westminster, no attempt was made anywhere in England during the Marian period to restore the bones or relics of the many saints that had been hidden away in Henry VIII's time. That was not the purpose of those charged with the Catholic restoration in England: their task was not the blind, reactionary return to former ways but the promotion of a new version of Catholicism that had absorbed the positive features of the Reformation.[38] 'The omission [to reinstate the remains] may seem hard to explain,' Moore conceded, 'but it appears to have occurred in fact.'[39]

Moore's final position was cautious but clear. He saw significant similarities between the events in Ravenna, Durham and Canterbury, albeit with gradations of probability.

> In the case of Dante, the proof of identity is assuredly complete; in that of St Cuthbert the strength of circumstantial evidence is all but irresistible; in that of St Thomas the conclusion remains, and ever must remain, doubtful. In my own mind the balance inclines very strongly to the side of its probability. Others will no doubt come to the opposite conclusion. I certainly do not think them unreasonable in doing so. I hope they will not think me unreasonable if I am disposed to come down with some confidence on the other side of the fence.[40]

With Moore's recruitment to the ranks of the 'believers' in the Becket hypothesis, the simple numerical balance of published opinion by about 1917 amounted to four 'believers' (Austin, Routledge, Thornton and Moore) and eight 'sceptics' (Sheppard, Venables, Morris, Arkasden, Milman, Beazeley, Vallance and Woodruff). By contrast, the crude balance of published opinion about the true fate of Becket's remains in 1538 amounted to six who held that they had been buried (Austin, Routledge, Thornton, Milman, Trice Martin and Moore), and only five who accepted the conventional wisdom that they had been burned (Sheppard, Venables, Beazeley, Morris and Arkasden).

Within a few years, however, a new publication was to change the balance of opinion and action appreciably.

Becket lies in Pontigny Abbey, ill from
excessive fasting, while the doctor examines
a specimen flask (from *Becket's Leaves*).

5   *Archiepiscopal Intervention*

It is not clear why, at this stage, archiepiscopal intervention in the debate should have occurred, but it did. At some time prior to 1920 the Archbishop of Canterbury, Randall Thomas Davidson, commissioned Canon Dr A.J. Mason to bring together all the relevant documents bearing upon the question of whether the bones discovered in the coffin in 1888 could have been those of St Thomas Becket. Ostensibly, the Archbishop's commission did not require Mason to reach an opinion about the identity of the bones. As will be seen, however, Mason adopted a very clear position on the identification of the remains; though whether in doing so he embarrassed the Archbishop by exceeding his brief is a matter of speculation.

The ecclesiastical background to Mason's commission was, in certain respects, similar to that in the late 1880s when the bones had first been found. The tensions between the evangelical and the catholic wings of the Church of England remained, and, as Davidson was well aware, the cry of 'no popery' still carried force.[1] In his first public action as Archbishop, in 1903, he had received a hundred members of parliament urging him to take effective action against the ritualists.[2] Indeed, the years before and immediately after the First World War were, in many respects, the heyday of Anglo-Catholicism.[3] The war itself had fuelled a demand for greater freedom in worship, and many service chaplains returning to the parishes were quite familiar and comfortable with such 'popish' practices as prayers for the dead.

In contrast to the dying years of the nineteenth century, the focus of contention in the opening years of the twentieth century was less upon ritual than upon the Book of Common Prayer, which had remained unchanged since 1661. Archbishop Davidson had responded to the concerns of the evangelicals by persuading the Prime Minister, Mr Balfour, to appoint a Royal Commission on Ecclesiastical Discipline. The Commission reported in 1906, recommending, among other things, a broadening in the laws governing the worship of the Church of England. In response, the Convocations of Bishops and Clergy began the long and complex process of revising the Book of Common Prayer.

The new, revised Prayer Book, which eventually came to parliament for ratification in 1927, was opposed by both the evangelical and the catholic wings of the Church: the former because it went too far in adopting the styles of Rome, the latter because it did not go far enough. The revisions were passed by the House of Lords but rejected by the Commons, the debate there eventually being swayed by the rhetoric of those evangelically-inclined members of parliament opposed to the changes. One speech, by the Scottish MP Rosslyn Mitchell, was said to have been especially effective for its familiar 'no popery' rhetoric.[4] In a single night the House of Commons undid the work of more than twenty years, suggesting that, however irrational it may have been in this particular context, the fear of Roman Catholicism ran much deeper than the leaders of the Church may have realised.

Tomb of Randall Thomas Davidson, Trinity Chapel.

Davidson himself was largely unmoved by the controversy over the revision of the Prayer Book, being more concerned about the quality of the Church's witness in the life of the nation. He was, however, well disposed towards the fledgling ecumenical movement and the dialogue with Rome. The sixth Lambeth Conference in 1920, at which he presided, had appealed for the reunion of Christendom on a much wider basis than had hitherto been possible; and Davidson had given his personal and friendly approval to a series of informal conversations held at Malines in Belgium between 1921 and 1925, between Anglican and Roman theologians. Davidson made it clear that the conversations were not a matter of negotiation, but rather of 'attempting a restatement of controversial questions and some elucidation of perplexities' (*Dictionary of National Biography*). He was too sensitive to the mood of the time to be seen to be offering too much support to the Anglo-Catholics.

This, broadly, was something of the background against which the Archbishop commissioned Canon Mason to assemble the documentary evidence about the skeleton in the crypt. It was, perhaps, curious that such a seemingly mundane and unimportant commission should have emanated from such a high office. Rather more understandable would have been a similar request from, say, the Dean of Canterbury. Perhaps the publication of Edward Moore's conclusions shortly after his death in 1916 had sparked off a controversy of such moment as to require its resolution as a matter of diplomatic urgency. If so, then Mason was an ideal choice for the assignment, for he too was well acquainted with high places.

Arthur James Mason, who was now to become a key figure in the quest for Becket's bones, was born in Wales in 1851 and educated at Repton School and Cambridge, where he graduated as eighth classic in the tripos of 1872. In his first post, as assistant master at Wellington College, he began his devoted and lifelong friendship with the headmaster, Edward White Benson, who, by 1888, when the bones were first found in the eastern crypt, had become Archbishop of Canterbury. Through the patronage of Benson, Mason became a canon of Truro Cathedral in 1878 where, as Archbishop Randall Davidson later recalled, 'he cut a lithe, spare figure, passing to and fro among the wind-swept villages of Cornwall, as if a mission priest had stepped out from the Celtic centuries into our own' (*Dictionary of National Biography*).

There then followed a parish appointment in the City of London and, with Benson now Archbishop, a canon's stall at Canterbury, where he became examining chaplain to the Archbishop. In 1895, however, Mason's scholarly reputation took him back to Cambridge, where he was elected as Lady Margaret Professor of Divinity and Professorial Fellow of

The murder of Thomas Becket. Reginald fitzUrse is distinguished by the bear on his shield. From an English psalter of *c.* 1190–1200.

Jesus College. Eight years later, in 1903, he became Master of Pembroke College, and in 1908 was appointed Vice-Chancellor of Cambridge University, a post he held for three years.

In 1912, with his health failing, Mason resigned the mastership of Pembroke College and withdrew to Canterbury, for which his affection had never dimmed. Apart from a short period spent in Alexandria in 1915, the rest of his life was spent there, engaged in the work of the Cathedral and in religious, educational and welfare matters in the city. He became a 'dear friend' of Edward Moore.[5] He lived long enough to see the revision to the Prayer Book rejected by the House of Commons, dying in Canterbury in 1928.

Ecclesiastically, Mason tended towards the upper end of the spectrum of churchmanship. He was convinced that the Church of England and its Prayer Book embodied the truth of catholic faith and tradition; nevertheless, he favoured the wider use of such practices as private confession and the ascetic life of religious communities. He was instinctively attracted to orthodoxy, ancient custom, stately worship and picturesque ceremonial. Behind the scenes of national and international ecclesiastical politics, where he moved freely for much of his life and was the intimate of archbishops, Mason was deeply involved in the ecumenical initiatives of the Church of England, including the discussions on reunion with the Roman Catholic Church.

This, then, was the man to whom, shortly after the end of the First World War, the Archbishop of Canterbury gave the commission to investigate the provenance of the skeleton in the crypt. Yet again, it was clear that these were not just any old bones. The passing years had done nothing to dull their extraordinary magnetism. The former Vice-Chancellor and Professor of Divinity at Cambridge gives every impression of having come to his task with a completely open mind. The result of his labour was a book that became without doubt the most wide-ranging review yet undertaken of the fate of Becket's remains.[6] Even those who subsequently disagreed with his conclusions held the work in high esteem. Hutton, for example, while rejecting Mason's eventual position, nevertheless described the book as 'the most scholarly and complete study',[7] praising its 'learning and candour and the interesting sidelights it sheds upon medieval and sixteenth century history'.[8] As a repository of the contemporary evidence about the relics of the saint, Mason's work has never been surpassed in importance and value.

Most of Mason's book was taken up with straightforward documentation rather than commentary or analysis. The first quarter of the book consisted of the contemporary accounts of the martyrdom given by five men who were present during the last hours of Becket: William of

What became of the Bones
of St Thomas?

A CONTRIBUTION TO HIS
FIFTEENTH JUBILEE

BY

ARTHUR JAMES MASON, D.D.
CANON OF CANTERBURY

CAMBRIDGE
AT THE UNIVERSITY PRESS
1920

Titlepage of *What Became of the Bones of St Thomas?* by Arthur James Mason (1920).

Canterbury, William fitzStephen, Benedict of Peterborough, John of Salisbury and Edward Grim. (See Barlow for a descriptive account of these sources and their reliability.)[9] The accounts are important for the evidence they offer about the precise manner of Becket's death, enabling a judgement to be formed on their compatibility with Thornton's account of the damage sustained by the '1888 skull'. The accounts, written originally in Latin, appear in the first four volumes of *Materials for the History of Thomas Becket, Archbishop of Canterbury*, published in the Rolls Series in seven volumes between 1875 and 1885. The remaining three volumes in *Materials* contain extensive correspondence pertaining to Becket.

The first of the five accounts is that of William of Canterbury, who was present at the beginning of the confrontation in the Cathedral between Becket and his murderers, but who fled up the stairs from the transept upon hearing fitzUrse's cry 'Strike! Strike!' After the martyrdom he began to compile a list of the miracles occurring at Becket's tomb in the crypt, which he was well placed to observe as he received the pilgrims there and heard their stories. Upon the completion of his account he presented a copy – rather surprisingly – to the King, and later wrote a history of the life of Becket.

The second witness, William fitzStephen, was a clerk in attendance on the Archbishop during the fateful day. He said of himself that 'I saw his passion at Canterbury, and many other things that are here written I saw with my eyes and heard with my ears; others again I learnt from those who witnessed them'. Since he claimed to have been present at the murder, fitzStephen's testimony is generally regarded as authoritative, although there is no independent evidence of its authenticity or even of his having been with Becket. His work, for example, is not mentioned in any of the other contemporary accounts or biographies of the Archbishop.

The third witness, Benedict, later to become Abbot of Peterborough, was a monk of the Priory of Christ Church at the time of the martyrdom and an acquaintance of Becket. He subsequently wrote an account of the life and death of the saint and of the miraculous cures associated with his tomb. His narrative shows evidence of the careful sifting and arrangement of the material he used.

John of Salisbury, one of the most eminent and able men of his age, was an intimate friend of Becket, having been his faithful companion and admirer during the Archbishop's exile in France between 1164 and 1170. He was present in the Cathedral at the time of the murder, but according to fitzStephen he left Becket before the knights entered from the cloisters. John's account of the actual killing is thus of little additional value to those of other witnesses who stayed with Becket to the end.

The last of the five accounts is that of Edward Grim, a secular clerk who was on a visit to Canterbury when the martyrdom occurred in December 1170. Not only was he present at the scene of the murder in St Benedict's Chapel, he actually tried to defend Becket from the first of the knights' blows, delivered by either fitzUrse or de Tracy. In the process, Grim suffered severe damage to his arm. According to his own account, he seems to have remained with Becket until the end, recording the last words spoken by the Archbishop before his death: 'For the name of Jesus and in defence of the church, I am ready to welcome death.'[10]

In addition to these narratives, Mason drew on three further sources from authors who had not actually been with Becket in his final hours but who later wrote their own accounts of his passion: Garnier, Herbert of Bosham, and Gervase. Garnier, a French clerk generally known as Garnier de Pont-Sainte Maxence, was the author of a life of Becket in

The sacrilege of the wound to the priestly tonsure is clearly shown in this Flemish miniature made for the English market around 1500.

French verse. Written between 1170 and 1176, it attests that its author took the greatest care to be accurate and complete. Garnier wrote much of it in Canterbury, checking the accuracy of what he had written with the prior and monks of Christ Church. His narrative is therefore a good account of local opinion and belief, dating back to within a short time of the event. Herbert of Bosham was a close and long-time acquaintance of Becket, and indeed was with him in Canterbury until a few days before his death. It was a matter of profound regret to Herbert for the rest of his life that he was not a witness to the martyrdom. His voluminous and prolix biography of Becket was written later than the other narratives, between about 1184 and 1187, but he is regarded as being well informed, with an eye for detail. Gervase was a monk of the Priory of Christ Church, born in about 1140, who meticulously chronicled most of the important events in the life of the community in his day, including his own eye witness account of the great fire of 1174 (see Chapter 1).

Having set out these assorted narratives of the killing of Thomas Becket, Mason then attempted to fashion them into a consistent account of the exact manner of Becket's death and the nature of the wounds inflicted upon his head. He was unable to do so. At best, the different testimonies could be melded into an impressionistic description of the manner of Becket's death that was likely to be true in its generalities but lacking in any agreement on details. The first of the knights' blows, delivered by either fitzUrse or de Tracy, did little damage to Becket, the force of it being taken by the arm of Edward Grim. Nor was it the last blow that killed him, for by this time he must have been all but dead. The force of this final strike, probably delivered by le Breton, was taken by the stone pavement, which broke off the point of his sword. Between these two hits, it is uncertain how many other blows reached Becket. Grim and Garnier (but not the others) reported a further blow, possibly delivered by fitzUrse, that left Becket still standing. It was the next strike, probably from de Tracy, that felled the Archbishop and may have killed him. After the final blow that caused le Breton's sword to shatter on the stone pavement, Hugh of Horsea (otherwise known as Hugh Mauclerc) placed his foot on Becket's neck, and with the point of his sword drew out the brains from a wound in the head and scattered them on the pavement. Mason thought from the evidence that Becket must have fallen on his right side, suggesting that the vital blow which felled him would have landed on the left side of his head – consistent with the pattern of damage to the skull found in the crypt.

When he turned to the nature of the wounds sustained by Becket, Mason could construct no clearer a picture. He reiterated the point made by previous writers that the 'corona' referred to in the contemporary

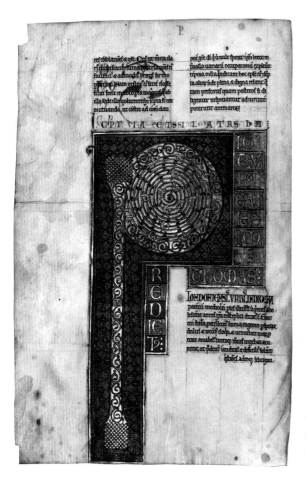

Decorated *Incipit* to a life of Thomas Becket by John of Salisbury, a life-long friend and leading English scholar of the time.

narratives must be understood as the part of Becket's head that had received the tonsure and unction, not as part of the cranial vault; but what happened to this corona was 'by no mean clear'[11] William of Canterbury did not mention it. William fitzStephen wrote that 'the whole crown of the head was cut off'. According to Edward Grim, the blow which wounded his own arm 'shore off the top of [Becket's] crown', and the last blow, when Becket was already prostrate, 'severed the crown from the head'. Benedict's evidence was that, after Becket had fallen, one of the knights 'cut off the greater part of the head'. Garnier said that the 'cupel' was taken off from the crown. Herbert of Bosham reported that a succession of blows 'severed the crown of the head from the head'.

The fullest account of the condition of Becket's head after the attack, Mason thought, was that of Gervase, the meticulous monkish recorder of

events in Christ Church Priory. Gervase had probably not witnessed the actual martyrdom, but he did see the body later. According to the Latin words used by Gervase in his account, some 'testulae' of Becket's head were cut off, the wound running down from the 'conus capitis' to the 'cella memorialis'. It was through this wound, Gervase said, that Hugh of Horsea had drawn out the brains with the point of his sword and scattered them, together with 'testulae' and blood, upon the pavement. Later Gervase added that 'the sacred blood, with the brain and testulae, was carefully collected and laid up'.[12]

Mason correctly thought that, in interpreting Gervase's narrative, a great deal hinged upon the precise medieval meaning of certain anatomical words, particularly 'testulae', 'conus capitis' and 'cella memorialis'. His conclusion, having sought expert help and advice, was that the 'conus capitis' referred simply to the top of the head; the 'cella memorialis' described the area at the back of the head above the nape of the neck; and 'testulae' were no more than splinters of bone. Unfortunately, Mason remarked, Gervase did not indicate the line of the cut between the 'conus capitis' and the 'cella memorialis'. If, as might naturally be assumed, it ran down the middle of the skull, then the skull discovered in the crypt could not be Becket's, for it was obviously not cloven in that way. However, a blow that fractured the skull in such a way could scarcely have severed the corona, whatever meaning might be given to it. Nor could it, as Gervase insisted, have enabled the sword that enlarged the wound to break upon the pavement, shearing off its point. 'To give any sense to Gervase's language,' Mason argued,

> we must, I think, understand him to mean that the line of the wound ran down along one side of the head, or the other side, between the points mentioned. According to the evidence, the dead or dying man lay on his right side. In this way, the left side of the skull, which had already been cloven by the blow that felled him, would again receive the first impact – probably from the half-handle of the sword – as the point snapped off on the stone. This would allow for the enlargement of the wound (to use Benedict's expression), and for the hacking off of 'testulae', chips and splinters of bone, and make it easier for the last assailant to strew the ground with them.[13]

It was in this way that Mason was able, in large measure, to reconcile the condition of the skull found in the crypt with the various accounts, particularly that of Gervase, of the state of Becket's head on the morning after his death. Mason further relied on Gervase to surmount the awkward fact that the skull in the crypt appeared to have sustained no

Becket's murder depicted in the Ramsey psalter of *c.* 1200. Reginald fitzUrse is identified by the bear on his shield and Edward Grim is on the right sustaining the wound to his arm.

damage to the area immediately around the crown. Gervase, he noted, gave no specific information about the corona that was supposed to have been severed. If any bony part of the cranial vault had been cut off, to Gervase it was only one of several 'testulae' or broken bits of bone. It cannot have been a large piece, for otherwise Gervase would scarcely have failed to write of it separately. 'From his silence,' Mason concluded, 'we should judge either that the corona, if detached at all, was put on again and buried with the rest of the head ... or that the name was afterwards given to one of the precious chips which at the time had nothing very remarkable about it to distinguish it from the rest.'[14]

The next section of Mason's book brought together the contemporary documentary evidence about the history of the saint's relics from the day of his burial (30 December 1170) to the destruction of the shrine by Henry VIII's Commissioners in September 1538. It included Benedict's description of the tomb in the crypt, eight separate accounts of the translation of the body from the tomb to the shrine in the Trinity Chapel on 7 July 1220, and a number of eye witness accounts of the various memorials and relics of the saint that were shown to pilgrims visiting the Cathedral prior to the Reformation. Of particular importance was the extended consideration given by Mason to what purported to be the relics of Becket's head and corona, which appear to have been on display in different parts of the Cathedral at different times and which pilgrims were invited to kiss before offering their gifts.

The third section of Mason's book dealt with the destruction of the shrine. It included, as well as the relevant sections of the contemporary chronicles of Wriothesley, Stow and Holinshed, a great deal of additional material about the King's purposes and policies in abolishing the monasteries, together with evidence about the fate of the shrines and tombs of other saints elsewhere, including St Richard at Chichester, St Hugh at Lincoln, St Cuthbert at Durham, and St William at York. Also included in this section of the book were Pope Paul III's bull of excommunication against the King in December 1538, the evidence of Cardinal Reginald Pole (the last Roman Catholic Archbishop of Canterbury) about the fate of Becket's remains, and extracts from relevant royal proclamations.

The last main section of Mason's book set out the contemporary material surrounding the discovery of the coffin in the crypt in 1888. Included here were some extracts from the report of the original Investigating Committee and of the surgeon who examined the bones, Mr Pugin Thornton. Several pages were filled with the letters written by Miss Agnes Holland to her friend at Oxford, Miss Lisa Rawlinson. This correspondence, extracts from which were quoted in Chapter 2, was apparently discovered by Mason and published here for the first time.

Reginald Pole, the last
Roman Catholic Archbishop
of Canterbury; after Titian,
c. 1558.

It was not until the final few pages that Mason allowed himself the
indulgence of speculating about the identity of the person whose bones
they might have been. Before revealing his position, Mason first
reviewed 'a few more facts which bear to some degree upon the question
of whose bones they were'.[15] In doing this, he again went over some of
the ground that had been mapped out by others in the debate since 1888.

Mason was evidently impressed by the fact that the eastern crypt, in
which the coffin was found, had been walled off in 1546 for the domestic
use of the first prebendary and had not been reopened to the public until
about 1838. The man to whom this crypt-cum-cellar was first allotted,
Richard Thornden, was a former monk of the Priory of Christ Church
who had attained high office in it. Although he accepted ordination in
the new Church of England as Bishop of Dover, Thornden remained

sympathetic to the Catholic cause, later restoring the Latin rite and gaining notoriety as a persecutor in the reign of Mary Tudor.[16] 'It would not be unnatural,' Mason observed, 'that a man of such character and history should contrive to gain possession of this portion of the crypt if he knew that it contained a hidden treasure like the bones of St Thomas.'[17]

Next Mason expressed the view that, if Becket's bones had been buried rather than burned when the shrine was destroyed in 1538, it need not have been the furtive act that most earlier commentators (including his colleague Dr Edward Moore) had assumed. The King was determined that, whatever happened to Becket's relics, they should never again become the focus of pilgrimage and veneration. This could have been assured, as it was at Durham, Lincoln and elsewhere, simply by colluding with the officials and monks of the priory in burying the saint's remains in an unmarked place. The monks, Mason suggested, probably allowed the Commissioners to find the bones untouched in the shrine and to burn instead some duplicate relics which had been kept elsewhere in the Cathedral. Among these colluding monks might well have been Richard Thornden, later to become the beneficiary of the walled-off crypt in 1546. These men, Mason observed, knew better than to divulge their secret.

Mason found no difficulty in reconciling the dimensions of the skeleton, as reported by Thornton, with the probable height and build of Becket in life. On the question of why, if the skeleton really was that of Becket, it had not been exhumed and reinstated during the reign of Mary Tudor, Mason offered the same simple, empirical rejoinder that Moore had deployed a few years earlier: this was not what had happened to saints' remains in the Marian period. With the exception of St Edward at Westminster, there was no known example of any such reinstatement. It may be unexpected, but that is how it was. 'There is therefore nothing to be surprised at if the bones of St Thomas were known to be in Bishop Thornden's cellar, and left there.'[18]

So Mason came finally to his brief conclusions. The bones discovered in 1888 were those of a man corresponding in age and height to Thomas Becket. They were the bones of one who appeared to have been killed by a blow to the left side of the head from a sharp-edged weapon. They had been removed from elsewhere, presumably prior to 1546, to the place in the eastern crypt where they were found in 1888. Unless they were known to be the bones of someone of importance, they would not have been moved, and certainly not to that particular place in the crypt. The historical evidence concerning Becket's death wounds was conflicting, and the best account of them, by the monk Gervase, made no mention of a separate corona. There was no direct evidence that the contents of Becket's shrine had been burned in 1538, merely, as Thomas Derby had written in 1539, that they had been 'taken away and bestowed in suche place as the same shuld cause no superstition afterwards' (see Chapters 4 and 8). Meanwhile, there was no place more suitable to bury the bones of St Thomas than the spot where the coffin had been discovered in 1888. 'These facts,' Mason concluded, 'seem to point to the conclusion that the bones in question are the bones of the great Archbishop.'[19]

But Mason (like all the other 'believers' since 1888) was to be proved wrong. In 1949 the Dean and Chapter decided to reopen not only the issue but also the coffin. The results were startling.

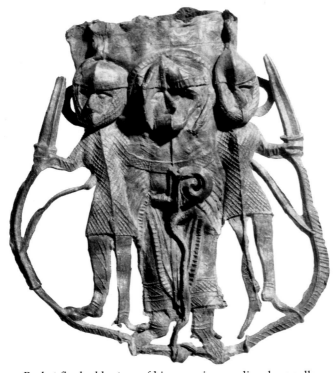

Becket flanked by two of his assassins; medieval ampulla.

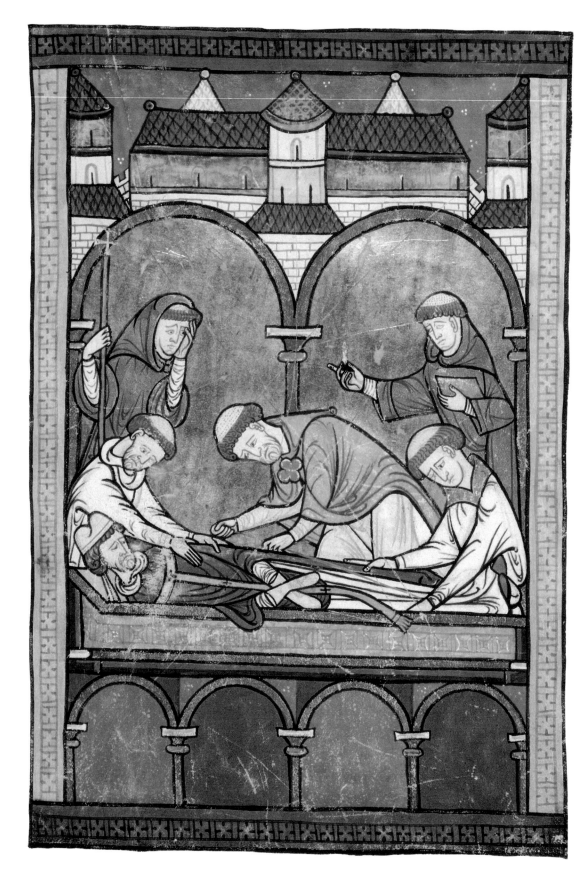

6   *The Grave Revisited*

T he grave in the eastern crypt was reopened on Monday, 18 July 1949, exactly 61 years and 159 days after it had been sealed on that February afternoon in 1888. At seven o'clock in the evening two workmen of the Chapter staff, Mr Shilling and Mr Baldock, began the task of chipping away the cement surrounding the huge slab. On this occasion there was no Miss Holland to witness the event, but some typewritten notes, presumably made by someone who was present, have been preserved in the Cathedral Archives.[1]

By 8.15 p.m. a small group of observers had assembled to witness the opening of the coffin. Perhaps not too dissimilar to their predecessors who had participated in much the same kind of ceremony in 1888, they included (in addition to Messrs Shilling and Baldock) Canon John Shirley, the Archdeacons of Canterbury and Maidstone, Professor A.J.E. Cave of the Anatomy Department at St Bartholomew's Hospital Medical College, Dr Jack Trevor of the Faculty of Archaeology at Cambridge University, a Mr Tophill, a Mr Anderson and Dr William Urry (then the Cathedral librarian). By the time the dignitaries arrived, the coloured edging around the slab had been chiselled out, and Shilling and Baldock were trying to lift the slab with crowbars. The crypt by this time was too dark to permit the work to proceed without artificial light, and a make-shift lamp was rigged up at the end of a flex plugged into the organ.

When the slab began to move just before 8.20, Mr Tophill went to summon the Dean, Dr Hewlett Johnson, who arrived on the scene at 8.30. At 8.25 the eastern end of the slab was lifted, and it was then possible to see through the gap to the lid of the wooden inner coffin that had been inserted inside the Portland stone coffin in 1888. There was a longitudinal crack in the lid. As the slab was raised further, iron piping was introduced to act as rollers, and the slab was pushed from above the coffin in a north-easterly direction to avoid the central Purbeck marble pillar in the aisle of the crypt. By now it was clear that the lid of the wooden coffin had sunk and split, and the bones could be glimpsed for the first time. An unpleasant smell oozed upwards from the hole. The slab was quickly removed from the site, and the coffin lay exposed to the gaze of the gathered spectators.

Becket is buried in his archiepiscopal vestments;
from an English psalter of *c*. 1200.

The broken lid of the coffin was lifted away, and the bones were seen to be positioned much as they had been at the first opening in 1888 (although, as noted in Chapter 2, no detailed record was made of the disposition of the bones before they were removed on that first occasion). They were arranged at the upper end of the coffin, not in anatomical order. The skull, still on the damp plaster mould around which it had been arranged by Mr Thornton, had fallen on to its right side, in a southerly direction. It rested on the stone pillow, cracked down the middle, as described in the report of the original Investigating Committee. The bottle that had been placed in the coffin in 1888 was discovered behind the skull, but it was found to be smashed, the contents saturated, and the writing all but illegible. It was not clear to the observers whether the extreme condensation on the bottle had been caused by moisture inside the coffin or, since it was a very humid evening, by its exposure to the ambient air.

Professor Cave and Dr Trevor quickly set to work on the bones, removing them from the coffin and laying them on sheets of paper on the floor of the crypt. In a move reminiscent of the 1888 drama, a large box was brought from Canon Shirley's house, into which the larger bones were placed, wrapped in paper. The skull and smaller bones were placed in smaller record boxes brought from the Cathedral Library. The rotten wood from under the inner coffin was put into another box for sifting. One plank from the coffin was left in the grave, together with the stone pillow. The remainder of the coffin was set aside for later disposal by the workmen. The Portland stone coffin in which the bones had been discovered in 1888, and into which the new oak coffin had been inserted at that time, was not removed from the ground, but its internal dimensions were measured by Dr Urry.[2] Everyone left the crypt at about 10.20 p.m. except for the workmen and Mr Anderson, who remained behind to close the grave and tidy up.

The decision of the Dean and Chapter to reopen the grave in 1949 seems, at face value, to have been quite out of keeping with the spirit of the times. The insatiable appetite of the Victorians for that sort of thing had long since given way to a more respectful and pacific attitude towards the dead. The decision was taken at a meeting of the Chapter on 5 February 1949 when, according to the minutes,

> Dr Shirley read a letter received from Mr A.B. Emden with regard to the inspection of the bones purported to be those of St Thomas. After discussion, Dr Shirley was asked to consult Mr J.C. Trevor of Cambridge and Professor A.J.E. Cave, St Bartholomew's Hospital, London, as to whether the proper date of the bones could be ascertained.[3]

John Shirley becomes, from now on, a significant figure in the story.[4] Born in 1890, he was educated at Oxford High School and Oxford University, where he was a student at St Edmund Hall between 1909 and 1912 when Dr Edward Moore was principal (see Chapter 5). After a number of teaching appointments, he read law and was called to the bar at Lincoln's Inn in 1920. In the following year he was ordained priest. Shirley returned to teaching, becoming headmaster of St Cuthbert's College, Worksop in 1925 and, ten years later, headmaster of the King's School, Canterbury and Canon Residentiary of the Cathedral. As headmaster, Shirley was fabulously energetic and successful; he also engaged himself fully in the life of the Cathedral and its Chapter during a period when, by virtue of his political sentiment and activities, the Dean of Canterbury (Dr Hewlett Johnson) was increasingly alienating himself from the sympathies of his colleagues. In consequence, Shirley seems to have assumed an ever more influential position within the Chapter, as is illustrated by the fact that it was he, rather than the Dean, who was the prime mover behind the initiative to reopen the grave in the eastern crypt.

The letter from Mr A.B. Emden, which seems from the *Minutes of the Canterbury Chapter* to have acted as some kind of catalyst in the decision, is intriguing. No copy of it can be traced in the archives either at Canterbury or at St Edmund Hall. Alfred Emden was a contemporary and intimate friend of Shirley.[5] Their paths crossed in several ways. Emden had been a pupil at the King's School, Canterbury (though not, of course, while Shirley was headmaster), and he was principal of St Edmund Hall, Oxford from 1929 to 1951, long after Shirley had left. Like Shirley, he was called to the bar, though he did not enter the Church. Emden was a distinguished historian, acquiring honours that included an honorary DLitt and Fellowships of the British Academy and the Royal Society of Arts.

Why did Emden write to the Chapter about a further inspection of the bones? What did he say? Was he merely offering a personal opinion that the time had come finally to lay to rest the rumours about their identity, or did he have other evidence about their provenance which might have justified the drastic step of reopening the grave? If so, what was that evidence, and was it connected in any way with the work of one of Emden's predecessors as principal of St Edmund Hall, Dr Edward Moore?

The only direct testimony about the reasoning behind the Chapter's decision to reopen the grave is that of Shirley himself. As he explained in an article in *The Times* in 1951, public opinion about the identity of the bones had hardened almost to the point where their identification as those of Becket was generally accepted. The Dean and Chapter, however, were 'not happy in this ascription, which might well have become, by constant repetition, avowed as fact'.[6]

A further possible reason is tantalisingly suggested in the pages of the *Minutes of the Canterbury Chapter* between 1946 and 1949. Throughout the autumn of 1946 the Chapter was engaged in discussions with Mr G.B. Beadle of Faith Craft-Works Ltd about the possibility of 'marking the burial place of St Thomas'. In October of that year, Mr Beadle was asked to produce a plan for some 'simple posts and cord' to mark the site.[7] Later that month the Chapter received Mr Beadle's design, but thought that 'it would be better if the posts were coloured'.[8] Mr Beadle submitted a revised design to the Chapter in November, but members deferred further consideration of the scheme until they 'had had an opportunity of inspecting similar enclosures in Westminster Abbey'.[9]

No further action appears to have been taken on the matter until May 1948, when the Chapter agreed that 'Messrs Seeley and Paget [a firm of architects in London] be asked to advise as to the best method of marking the burial site of St Thomas of Canterbury'.[10] In June the Dean reported that the architects had been commissioned to prepare a scheme,[11] and in August a letter to the Dean from Seeley and Paget spoke of their intention to 'present our design for a "hearse" to protect the believed resting place of Becket's bones'. The letter added that 'the design itself is fully complete and is now being drawn out clearly to show the effect in perspective'. The Chapter met with the architects in September, presumably to discuss their progress,[12] and in the following month a design was submitted by them 'for the Tomb of St Thomas of Canterbury'.[13] One year later, in October 1949, a letter was read to the Chapter from Mr Paul Paget 'with regard to . . . the protection of the believed resting place of Becket's bones', and Shirley undertook to meet Lord Mottinstone and Mr Paget later that month.[14]

None of these minutes identifies the actual site in question. They refer variously to 'the burial place of St Thomas', 'the burial site of St Thomas of Canterbury' and 'the believed resting place of Becket's bones'. These sites may not have been one and the same, although common sense suggests that they probably were. The place in which the Chapter believed the bones of Becket to be resting was most likely to have been the grave in the eastern crypt, though the minutes do not provide conclusive identification. There are other possible locations, some of which are discussed in Chapter 8. If, however, the site in question was indeed the grave in the eastern crypt, then the rather startling fact emerges that, at least until October 1949, the Dean and Chapter were accepting the '1888 bones' as being genuinely those of Becket. They were even preparing to acknowledge their acceptance publicly, through the erection of a structure, described variously as a hearse and as a tomb, to protect the site. This fact sits somewhat uneasily with Shirley's later assertion in *The Times* in August 1951 that the Dean and Chapter had 'not been happy in this ascription'.[15]

If it is a correct inference from the *Minutes of the Canterbury Chapter* that, until late in 1949, the Dean and Chapter believed the true remains of Becket to be resting in the grave in the eastern crypt, then the decision early in 1949 to reopen the grave for the purpose of identifying the contents is puzzling. After all, the Dean and Chapter had had twenty-eight years since the publication of Mason's book in which to consider their position, and in October 1948 they were actually looking at the design that they themselves had commissioned for 'the Tomb of St Thomas of Canterbury'. Why, then, only a few months later in February 1949, were the Dean and Chapter contemplating the reopening of the grave for the purpose of identifying the bones? It was a serious and highly unusual step to take, unlikely to have been prompted by a mere sense of curiosity.

The correct answer may well be the obvious one – that the Chapter felt it prudent to carry out a last-minute check, before it was too late, to ensure that an embarrassing misattribution was not about to be made. If, as the minutes suggest, the Dean and Chapter were contemplating the erection of a tomb (presumably, that is, some kind of vessel to contain the bones), then sooner or later the bones themselves would come under the critical gaze of modern science, with obvious discomfiture to the Cathedral authorities were it to transpire that they were patently not those of the saint. Yet if this was the real reason for reopening the grave at this particular time, why did Shirley later assert that the Dean and Chapter had never been happy with the idea that these were Becket's remains, and wished to prevent it from taking ineradicable root in the public mind? Was it merely a *post hoc* way of avoiding the mildly awkward admission that the Dean and Chapter had indeed made a mistake? Or did the Chapter come into possession of new information that made the reopening of the grave imperative for quite other reasons? And if so, was that information related to the letter that the Chapter had received from Mr Emden and discussed just prior to their decision on 5 February 1949?

The morning after their re-exhumation, on 19 July 1949, the bones were taken by Professor Cave to the Anatomy Department at St Bartholomew's Hospital Medical College, where they remained under examination for two years. In 1951 a report was submitted by Professor Cave to the Dean and Chapter, a copy of which was placed in the Cathedral Library.[16] The Chapter expressed the hope that a full report would be published in due course;[17] but no such general publication ensued, and it seems that the only public communication about Professor Cave's report was made in the short article by Canon Shirley that appeared first in *The Times* and later in *Archaeologia Cantiana*.[18] The article was a perfectly accurate summary of the main points of the Cave report – indeed, much of it was taken up with direct quotations from the report. But as will be seen, Shirley failed to draw out the implications of some of Professor Cave's findings.

There are hints in the archival material that certain loose ends were still being pursued behind the scenes even after the submission of Professor Cave's report to the Dean and Chapter in May 1951. A letter from Canon Shirley to Dr Urry in January 1952 shows that another member of the investigating team, Dr Jack Trevor of Cambridge University, was preparing his own separate report,[19] though no trace of any such report has come to light, and Trevor's role in the proceedings remains unclear. In the letter, Shirley asked Urry whether any evidence was to be found in the Archives of the age at death of William de Audeville, the Abbot of Evesham who died in Canterbury in 1159, and who was apparently buried in the precise place in which the coffin had been found in 1888 (see Chapter 4).

The eventual fate of Professor Cave's report to the Dean and Chapter is mildly interesting: it disappeared. Attempts to locate a copy of it in Canterbury in 1993 came to naught. It was to be found neither in the Cathedral Library, nor in the Archives, nor among the records of the Receiver General. It was not with the personal papers of the Dean of the day (Dr Hewlett Johnson) in the library of the University of Kent. Eventually, however, a copy was obtained from Professor Cave himself, then aged 93 and living in north London. By good fortune he had retained it among his personal papers, though had he died before the enquiry was made, the last extant copy of his report might have gone with him.

As with the recruitment of his counterpart sixty years earlier (Mr Pugin Thornton, MRCS), the reasons for Professor Alexander Cave's involvement in the re-examination of the skeleton are not clear. He must have been sounded out, or at least covertly assessed, before the Chapter took the decision in February 1949 to consult him on the matter; but he is not known to have had any prior connections with Canterbury – or, for that matter, with St Edmund Hall. Cave was, however, an eminent scientist, and he may simply have been the best person in the field. He was born and educated in Manchester, graduating in medicine from Manchester University. At the time of his summons from the Dean and Chapter he had been Professor of Anatomy at St Bartholomew's Hospital Medical College for three years. He was a past president of the Linnean

Society and an authority on mammalian morphology, physical anthropology and medical history – precisely the expertise required to fulfil the Dean and Chapter's commission.

Professor Cave's report on his examination of the bones, dated 21 May 1951 and signed by him alone, was thirty-one pages long and typewritten in double spacing. In the covering letter accompanying the report, Cave defined his brief as that of

> the possible determination, in the light of present-day scientific knowledge, of any intrinsic evidence which might establish, or suggest, the identity of these remains as the relics of St Thomas of Canterbury.

That he had decisively to refute any such identity was, he confessed, a personal disappointment; but he quite properly added that the issue had to be resolved solely on the evidence afforded by the skeleton itself.

The first point to which Cave drew attention in his report was the poor condition of the bones. Interestingly, the plaster mould on which Thornton had mounted the remnants of the skull in 1888, and which had been buried with bones, had remained wet and plastic; but this had had unfortunate effects. By introducing moisture into the sealed coffin, the decaying process of the bones had been accelerated and many of them had been attacked by a fungal organism. Mould growths had occurred in whitish patches on many of the bones, and some (especially the nasal bones and much of the pelvis) had disintegrated upon even the gentlest handling.

The mould growth was removed, the bones were cleaned and slowly dried, and the long, exacting business began of identifying all the bone fragments, many of which were no more than chips and splinters. Large parts of the skeleton were missing, including all the base of the skull, most of the face, and parts of the pelvis and spine. The reconstruction of the skeleton was therefore a lengthy process during which a few mistakes were inevitably made. Eventually, however, all the fragments were restored to their correct anatomical position save only three or four insignificant flakes. The skull posed particular problems of reconstruction. A lot of it was missing, including the entire cranial base, most of the orbital walls, the right half of the face, the nasal fossa walls, and part of the vault. But at last the reconstruction was completed, using wax to fill the spaces left by the missing bones and fragments.

Cave turned his attention first to the skull, since this was always likely to be the critical part of the skeleton for the purpose of identification. It was this that provided the clearest evidence (though, as will be seen, not the only evidence) that the skeleton could not have been Becket's. The reconstructed cranium was unmistakably male in all its features, and had belonged to a large and robust man. The condition of the cranial sutures strongly suggested a man at the beginning of his seventh rather than his sixth decade. The man had had a normal and healthy set of teeth at the time of his death, though only five then remained.

Turning to the celebrated 'corona', Cave first rehearsed the argument about its importance. The blow that killed Becket, he asserted, had detached the crown of his skull, the earlier blows having wounded the soft tissues only. Therefore, he maintained, 'the authentic relic must show unmistakable evidence of instrumental breakage and detachment of the uppermost portion of the cranial vault'.[20] Now, among the numerous pieces of bone from the cranium Cave did indeed find a large upper calvarial fragment of irregular and angulated pentagonal outline. It was this, he thought, that had been interpreted in 1888 as the 'corona' of Becket's skull. It had certainly been so mounted on the plaster block by Thornton as to appear isolated from the rest of the vault. Indeed, Cave detected a hitherto unknown element of Victorian melodrama: the plaster underlying the gap that separated the piece of bone from the rest of the skull had been tinted red.

Cave was absolutely sure, however, that Thornton's original reconstruction of the skull had been fundamentally flawed: in fact, this piece of bone fitted naturally into its place in the rest of the skull, and was nothing more than a large piece of the top of the skull that had become detached as a result of damage occurring after death. The edges of the bone were jagged, angulated and irregular, and they showed no evidence of contact with a cutting instrument. Rather, they displayed the 'ordinary, natural fracture-surfaces characteristic of buried skulls of all periods and tally exactly with archaeological material of Romano-British, Anglo-Saxon and XVIIIth century date, with which they have been compared'.[21]

Had the fractures been caused by a cutting instrument before death, then a certain amount of bony tissue would have been missing from the surface edges; but this was not the case. They were obviously post-mortem fractures, caused by the disintegration of the entire cranium as a result of natural decay and the pressure of impacted earth. 'It is quite certain,' Cave concluded, 'that [this piece of bone] was not detached instrumentally from the living head. It cannot therefore be the "corona" of St Thomas, and hence the skeleton cannot be identified with the martyr's remains.'[22]

It may be argued that Cave's criterion of authenticity for the skull, namely that a section of bone should have been cut off from the rest of the cranium vault, was too stringent. It certainly took no account of the view of Mason and others, based partly upon the contemporary witness of the monk Gervase, that the 'corona' denoted not a segment of bone but the consecrated tonsure, and that the real skull need not necessarily have been damaged in this particular way. Yet Cave's rejection of the skull as being that of Becket did not rest only upon the fate of the 'corona': he explicitly stated that no ante-mortem wounds had been made with a cutting instrument *anywhere* about the skull:

> All the cracks, breaks, fractures and erosions are most emphatically of a post-mortem nature.[23]

This observation must be regarded as conclusive: whatever the precise pattern and sequence of injuries sustained by Becket's head at the time of his death, it is beyond question that some terrible and fatal blows landed upon it, fracturing it at least to the extent of enabling Hugh of Horsea to insert the point of his sword and draw out some of the brains. It would require the most violent distortion of the contemporary evidence to argue that a skull displaying no traces whatsoever of ante-mortem injury could be that of the martyr.

Having decisively and finally refuted the Becket hypothesis, much of the remainder of Cave's report appears as an anti-climax, consisting as it does of a detailed and technical account of the rest of the skeleton. Many of the bones had suffered from decay and fragmentation, but sufficient remained to permit a reasonable description of the man whose skeleton they had constituted. The bones could, in Cave's opinion, be confidently dated to the medieval period, possibly the twelfth century. (The report gives no indication of how the dating was done, and it should perhaps be regarded as nothing more than an informed guess.) The man had been mature in age at the time of his death, possibly even elderly. The condition of the thyroid cartilage, the cranium, the spinal column and the teeth suggested an age between a low of 45 and a high of 60 or more. The evidence of the skeleton could be consistent with an age of 52 at the time of death (the probable age at which Becket had died), but Cave's 'distinct impression' was of a man nearer the age of 60, or even more.

The man had been of robust build and about five feet eight inches in height. (Thornton's estimate of the height of the skeleton, upon which so much of the debate had hinged during the previous sixty years, had been hopelessly exaggerated.) He had probably been right-handed. There was evidence that he had suffered from osteoarthritis, particularly in the spine. Many bones from the hands and feet were missing, as also were the atlas, the upper thoracic vertebrae, many ribs, parts of the scapulae and sternum, and much of the face and base of the skull. All but five of the teeth were missing, having been removed from the skull after death. All the damage to the skeleton had been caused after death, much of it due to natural fracturing and disintegration resulting from an earlier burial in earth. Some damage, however, may well have been caused during the removal of the skeleton from the coffin in 1888.

Thus far, Professor Cave's report contained nothing that might suggest any unusual or inexplicable features surrounding the discovery of the skeleton in its ill-suited coffin. On page 22, however, there was the arresting observation that, *in addition to the bones of the skeleton, the coffin had also been found to contain an assortment of other bones, mostly animal ones.* They included a canine tooth and phalanx of a pig; fragments of the vertebrae and premaxillae of a sheep or goat; the distal tibial epiphysis, cuneiform and rib fragments of a small ox; the femur of a small bird; part of the os calcis of an unidentified mammal; and various other mammalian bone fragments. There was also an incomplete upper vertebra from another, smaller human skeleton.

Most of these bone fragments were probably very small (though Cave did not indicate their size), but it is nevertheless odd that they received no mention in either of the 1888 reports. The original Investigating Committee had certainly noted that the coffin contained 'much earthen debris',[24] which, according to Thornton, had been 'carefully sifted'.[25] It is almost inconceivable that the extraneous bones went unnoticed, and indeed Miss Holland, in a letter to Canon Mason in March 1915, observed that 'a few small bones were left lying upon the floor of the coffin'.[26] Yet this observation was not included in the two formal reports that were submitted to the Dean and Chapter, so it was not available to those who subsequently speculated on the possible identity of the coffin's contents. Had it been, the implications to be drawn from the presence of the extraneous fragments of bone might have been realised, and the debate might have taken a rather different course.

Professor Cave himself helpfully highlighted the significance of the presence of the additional bones: *the skeleton had originally been buried elsewhere, in a recognised burial place, and had been exhumed, along with some of the surrounding soil containing the bone fragments of other people and animals buried nearby, before being deposited in the coffin in the crypt where it was found in 1888.* Moreover, as the presence of the earthen debris in the coffin indicated, the skeleton had been buried directly in the earth, not in a coffin or other container. Other pieces of evidence supported this startling conclusion. The condition of some of the bones was typical of 'grave-weathering'; the crushing and warping of the skull had been caused by the pressure of impacted earth; and many of the smaller bones

104

of the hands and feet, which would have become separated from the remainder of the skeleton during a prolonged period of burial in the earth, were missing. In these respects the skeleton compared exactly with buried human remains of various periods, from Neolithic to eighteenth century.

Not only had the skeleton been buried in the earth in another grave-yard prior to its exhumation and reburial in the crypt, but *the earlier burial had been of a complete human corpse, not of a collection of bones.* The evidence for this was clear and dramatic: many of the bones, particularly in the regions of the pelvis, femur, patella and tibia, had been damaged by spade-cuts which could only have been inflicted upon them while in their correct anatomical position with each other. What had been buried was a body; what had been exhumed were the skeletal remains of that body, in which the bones had been in their correct positions when damaged by the spades of those who had dug them up. As Cave himself put it,

> the incidence of the spade cuts shows the bones to have occupied, in the earth, their proper anatomical positions. The burial was that of an intact corpse and not the hurried inhumation of bones previously preserved as relics . . . . Buried osseous relics would never have assumed their intimate and proper anatomical relationships, no matter how thoroughly such might have been attempted, and the attempt (if made) was bound to failure from the very imperfect scientific knowledge of the day.[27]

The fact that the skeleton had originally been buried in earth as part of a whole corpse, not as a collection of bones, was further proof against the Becket hypothesis, for there is no evidence of his body ever having been buried directly in earth. After his death his body was contained first in a marble coffin, then in a wooden chest, and finally in the feretrum inside the shrine in the Trinity Chapel (Chapter 1). Even if it is held that his remains were committed to an earth burial when they were removed from the shrine in 1538, they could still not be those discovered in the coffin in the crypt; for as Cave pointed out, it is inconceivable that the monks (or whoever carried out the hypothesised deed) could have placed the bones in the earth in precisely the same relative positions that they would have occupied in the living body.

Professor Cave then offered one final important deduction about the history of the skeleton from his observations of it: *prior to its being placed in the coffin in the crypt, it had been exhumed in great haste, or with little care, or both.* The phrase chosen by Cave to describe the manner of the exhumation was that it had been done with 'gross . . . and destructive carelessness'.[28] The extensive damage caused to many of the bones by the spadework, the absence of such a large part of the skeleton, and the inclusion of a good deal of extraneous matter with the bones all pointed towards a hasty and furtive act, in which respect for the remains was either unnecessary or impossible. 'The exhumation,' Cave reported,

> was conducted with such apparent carelessness as to create the impression that the operation was not the deliberate excavation of known remains from a known site, but rather the accidental uncovering of a human burial during some digging operation. The deliberate search for, and excavation of, a known burial would surely have been conducted with greater care, both in the digging out of the skeleton and in the securing of all the bones. The breaking of so many of the bones and the leaving behind of so much of the skull, spine, hands and feet, may indicate an accidental rather than a deliberate exhumation.[29]

It is perhaps worth summarising, as succinctly as possible, the conclusions that Professor Cave reached about the skeleton that he spent two years examining, for they pose some intriguing but difficult questions about its identification. All of these conclusions were reported by Cave with a high degree of confidence, and with no trace of doubt or caution.

The skeleton, though emphatically not that of Thomas Becket, had once belonged to a large and robust adult male, possibly nearer 60 than 50 years of age.

The skeleton showed no signs of damage prior to death that might have been caused instrumentally. Though it was extensively fractured and fragmented, all the damage sustained by the skeleton could be attributed to natural decay, or to the effects of earth burial, and to breakages caused instrumentally after death.

Prior to their removal to the coffin in the crypt, the bones had been buried for some time directly in the earth, possibly in a recognised burial ground.

The earlier burial in earth had been of a complete corpse in which all the bones had been in their correct anatomical relationship with each other. The burial had not been that of a collection of bones or relics.

The bones had been dug up from the ground, prior to their placement in the coffin in the crypt, in great haste or with little care.

The bones were returned to Canterbury in 1951.[30] In June of that year a leaden box was made, the bones were placed reverently in it, and the lid was sealed in the presence of Canon Shirley. They were buried, for at least the third time in their existence, by Shirley on the evening of Friday, 15 June 1951, presumably in the Portland stone coffin that had remained in its usual position in the eastern crypt, between the westernmost two of the three Purbeck marble pillars. The grave was sealed with a plain, unmarked slab set flush with the level of the floor. There the bones have remained, undisturbed, to the present time. The significance of the slab is explained in various ways by the Cathedral guides to the few visitors who enquire. Some of the explanations that can be overheard are incorrect; some are correct as far as they go; none, understandably, conveys the excitement and challenge of the question: if not Becket's bones, whose are they?

Before engaging with that question, a curious little postscript must be added to the reburial of the bones in 1951: not all of them were replaced in the coffin. One tooth remained on the surface – probably the right upper canine tooth – and it now resides in the Cathedral Archives in a registered envelope postmarked Cambridge, 2 January 1951. The envelope, presumably containing the tooth, was sent originally by Dr Jack Trevor (a member of the scientific group that examined the skeleton) to Dr Gosta Gustafson, in Malmö, Sweden. Accompanying the envelope in the Archives is an anonymous handwritten note, undated and unaddressed, but carrying the initials 'NS'. It reads:

> This is one of the four teeth which the skeleton in the East Crypt was found to have on the occasion of our opening the tomb. You might like it in the relics and treasures of the Library. I have guarded it all the time – and after all, it might be a Saint's tooth.

The explanation is probably quite straightforward. Dr Gustafson was an acknowledged international expert on dating the age of death from teeth,[31] and Dr Trevor was presumably tasked with sending him one of the teeth for this very purpose. (If Gustafson ever offered an opinion on the age of the man at the time of his death, no record of it appears to exist; nor was his name mentioned in Professor Cave's report.) Gustafson, it may be assumed, retained the tooth beyond the time of the reburial in June 1951, but did eventually return it to Cambridge where it came in to the care of 'NS'. The identity of 'NS' is not absolutely clear, but it is probably the Very Reverend Norman Sykes, a close acquaintance of Canon Shirley. Sykes had a very distinguished academic career as an ecclesiastical historian in the Universities of London (1931–44) and Cambridge (1944–58) before becoming Dean of Winchester in 1958. Sykes must have kept possession of the tooth before handing it over to the Cathedral Archives some time before his death in March 1961.

A visual examination of the tooth by a dentist has revealed nothing that might be of any value in identifying the skeleton. If the tooth has any utility at all, it lies in the fact that the skeleton may be capable of being dated, using carbon-dating techniques, without resort to any further opening of the coffin. It is possible, though not certain, that knowledge of the approximate date of the skeleton could aid speculation about the identity of the man whose bones these had once been.

But who might that man have been? And what connection, if any, did he have with Becket?

Becket on horseback, denoting his fame
as a traveller and horseman; a medieval
pilgrim's badge.

7   *Burned or Buried?*

lthough Professor Cave's report was never published, its deci-
sive refutation of the Becket hypothesis, communicated to the
world through Canon Shirley's article in *The Times* in August
1951, effectively ended any extensive public debate about the bones for
over thirty years. The article attracted only one letter;[1] Cave's report
passed out of public memory; the tooth returned from Sweden came into
the safe keeping of 'NS'; and only the occasional member of the public
continued to be confused about the contents of the grave in the eastern
crypt.[2] The story of the find in 1888 was recounted in an article in the
Canterbury Cathedral Chronicle in 1981,[3] but, since the author had presumably not had access to the Cave report, she raised none of the intriguing
questions highlighted by it.

In the mid-1980s two books might have resurrected the question of the
fate of Becket's relics, though in fact they did not. In 1985 James Bentley's
Restless Bones described the events of 1888 in some detail, but failed to
mention the re-exhumation of the bones in 1949, leaving his readers with
the impression that they might, after all, have been those of the saint.[4] In
the same year, David Sox's *Relics and Shrines* cited an unnamed source of
information that Becket's episcopal ring had been found in the coffin in
1888 and that the skeleton had actually been reinterred in the Chapel of
St Mary Magdalene in the north transept of the crypt, next to the
unidentified slab embossed with the cross of Canterbury.[5] Neither claim
appears to be supported by the contemporary evidence.

In 1990 the question of the fate of Becket's bones surfaced again in the
shape of a tense 'whodunnit' novel set in the precincts of Canterbury
Cathedral and centred on the discovery of an ancient coffin in the crypt
containing what were thought to be the remains of the saint.[6] Much
was made in the novel of the political consequences of the find: the
fictional Dean in the story was of the strong opinion that, if authenticated as those of Becket, the remains in the coffin might prove to be an
important symbol around which Roman Catholic aspirations could
assemble, threatening the very survival of the Church of England. In the
event, the coffin was found to contain nothing more than a collection of
animal bones – a curious turn of the author's imagination in the light of

the Cave report, which appears at that time not to have been publicly accessible. The bones were explained in the novel as a decoy, set up by the monks in 1538, to divert the attention of any enquiring Commissioners away from the place where the true remains of Becket had been secreted.

Yet in some ways it is curious that the Cave report should have stilled any serious debate about the skeleton in the crypt, for all it showed was that these particular bones could not have been Becket's. The questions still remained: whose bones were they? And what happened to the true remains of the saint? As an anatomist, Professor Cave was able to throw light on neither question – though that did not deter him from speculating on them in his report. That these questions seem to have faded from public debate may be due as much as anything to the way in which the Cave report was summarised by Shirley in his article in *The Times*. For while he accurately presented the evidence that led Cave so decisively to reject the skeleton as that of Becket, he failed to raise the obvious question that would occur to any reader of the report: how did these particular bones, with their highly unusual history, come to be buried a few inches beneath the surface in a makeshift coffin in a site most intimately connected with St Thomas Becket? Nor did Shirley draw attention to the equally obvious question: if these particular bones were not those of the saint, what happened to the real ones in 1538, and do they still exist?

The answers to these two questions may be connected. If Becket's remains were really burned in 1538, then there is no further interest in them, and the identity of those discovered in the eastern crypt must be considered a puzzle in its own right. If, on the other hand, the remains were not burned in 1538, then the treatment accorded to them might in some way be linked to the coffin in the crypt and its contents. Before considering the identity of the skeleton in the crypt, the prior question must be addressed of the fate of Becket's relics when his shrine was destroyed. Were the bones burned or were they not? What actually happened in September 1538?

It was in that month that the Royal Commissioners for the Destruction of Shrines, under the supervision of Dr Richard Layton, then Archdeacon of Buckingham, arrived in Canterbury.[7] Layton had earlier served Wolsey as a zealous and sycophantic Commissioner in the suppression of the monasteries, and he could be trusted to do what was expected of him. He was a man of coarse and evil mind, quite prepared to use deceit and treachery in the pursuit of his goals.[8] As a Commissioner for the suppression of the monasteries he had brought false accusations against the monks even in monasteries where nothing was amiss. Later in 1539,

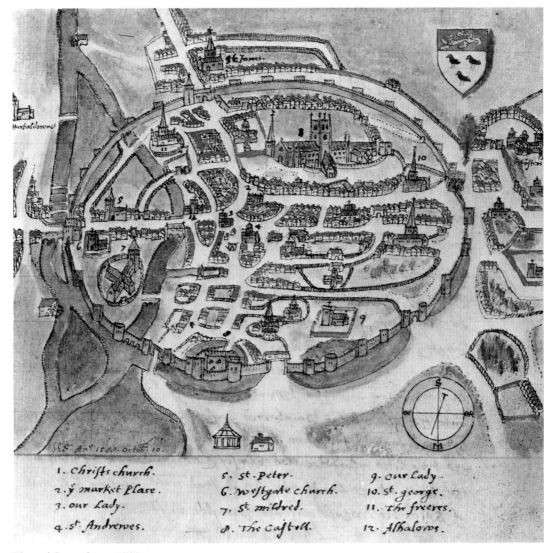

Plan of Canterbury, 1588.

upon becoming Dean of York, he marked his accession to the deanship by pawning the plate belonging to the Chapter.

Layton was no stranger to Canterbury, and he was well acquainted with the shrine of St Thomas. Three years earlier, in October 1535, he had supervised its protection when it had been threatened with fire. At the time, Layton was staying in the lodgings at Christ Church Priory, having brought to the prison there the Abbot of the Premonstratensian Abbey of Langdon, in Kent, whom he had caught *in flagrante delicto* with his mistress.[9] At one o'clock in the morning of 26 October, Layton, roused from his room in the lodgings by one of his servants, found the rush matting in the dining chamber where he had earlier taken supper on fire. He summoned help from the town, but before the ladders and buckets could arrive the building was engulfed in flames. Fearful for the safety of the priory's treasures, Layton made for the Cathedral. His actions there were later reported in a letter to Thomas Cromwell.

> As soon as I had set men to quench and to labour, I went into the church and there tarried continually, and set four monks with bandogs [a cross between a pit bull terrier and a Rottweiler] to keep the shrine of St Thomas Becket, and put the sexton in the revestry

Portrait of Thomas Cromwell (1485?–1540), after Holbein.

EARL OF ESSEX.

The two graves in the crypt, adjoining the Chapels of St Mary Magdalen and St Nicholas.

there to keep the jewels; and I walked continually in the church above; and set monks in every quarter of the church with candles, and sent for the abbot of St Augustine's [abbey] to be there within, in a readiness to have taken down the shrine and to have sent all the jewels into St Augustine's; but as it chanced there is no harm done there .... No plate nor nothing lost.[10]

Both the King (Henry VIII) and his principal minister and Lord Privy Seal, Thomas Cromwell, were in the neighbourhood of Canterbury when Layton and the Commissioners arrived in September 1538, which suggests that their wishes in the matter were strictly carried out. The content of those wishes, however, is not clear, for every authentic record of the demolition of the shrine has perished.[11] There was no general Act of Parliament dealing with the disposal of shrines and relics, nor any injunction on the matter from the King.[12] All that seems to exist is a general letter of command from the King, issued to the bishops through Archbishop Cranmer in October 1541, for the removal of any shrines, monuments and the like that still remained in the churches.[13] The letter noted that the King had earlier 'caused the images and bones of such as they [the people] resorted and offered unto, with the ornaments of the same ... to be taken away'. Now, however, the King

> has lately learnt that shrines, coverings of shrines and monuments of such things yet remain in sundry places, and therefore commands forthwith to search his cathedral church and if any such thing remains, to take it away.

The new injunction did not specifically include the relics of the saints, and no particular method of dealing with the shrines, coverings and monuments was mentioned. The phrase 'taken away' may be held to mean 'burned', but that would not be a common-sense interpretation.

The destruction of the shrines was carried out by local Commissioners acting under the authority of the Lord Privy Seal. Among other things, they 'disgarnished' and disposed of any shrines, bones, images, icons, relics and the like. No copy of the Commission for Canterbury has been found.[14] Commissions for other places do exist, however, and they show a common form. The Commission for Chichester, issued at Hampton Court on 14 December 1538 and signed by Thomas Cromwell, required the Commissioners to

> take and convey to the Tower of London the bones, shrine, etc. now in Chichester Cathedral, of a certain bishop of the same which they call

St Richard, and to see the place of the shrine destroyed, with all other images in that church whereabout there is any notable superstition.[15]

The shrine was destroyed six days later, on 20 December, and large quantities of gold, silver, ornaments and other jewels were removed, including 57 pieces of silver and gilt actually in the coffin with St Richard's bones.[16] The treasures were taken to the Tower of London,[17] but no record has survived about the manner of the disposal of the saint's remains. This, it appears, was left to the discretion of the Commissioners.

At Lincoln, where the shrines of St Hugh and St John of Dalderby stood, explicit permission was given for the exercise of local discretion. In this case the Commission, issued at Westminster on 6 June 1540, required the Commissioners (Dr George Hennage and others) to

take down and convey to the Tower of London a certain shrine and divers feigned relics and jewels in Lincoln Cathedral, by which simple people are deceived and brought into superstition and idolatry, together with all superfluous jewels, plate, copes, and the like, at their discretion.[18]

As at Chichester, no orders were issued for the disposal of the saints' remains, and their fate is not recorded.

A very similar pattern of events occurred at Winchester, where the shrine of St Swithin was destroyed on 21 September 1538. The story is recounted in a letter written to Thomas Cromwell by three of the Commissioners: Richard Pollard, Thomas Wriothesley and John Williams:

About three o'clock this Saturday morning, made an end of the shrine here at Winchester. There was no gold, nor ring, nor true stone in it, but all great counterfeits .... The altar will be worth taking down, but it is such a piece of work that they cannot finish it before Monday night or Tuesday morning; which done we intend ... to sweep away all the rotten bones that be called relics; which we may not omit lest it should be thought we came more for the treasure than for avoiding the abomination of idolatry.[19]

That the bones of St Swithin were to be 'swept away' does not obviously suggest that the Commissioners intended to burn them; yet it seems that whatever was done at Winchester differed in some respect from the Commissioners' actions at Canterbury. Writing to Cromwell a few days

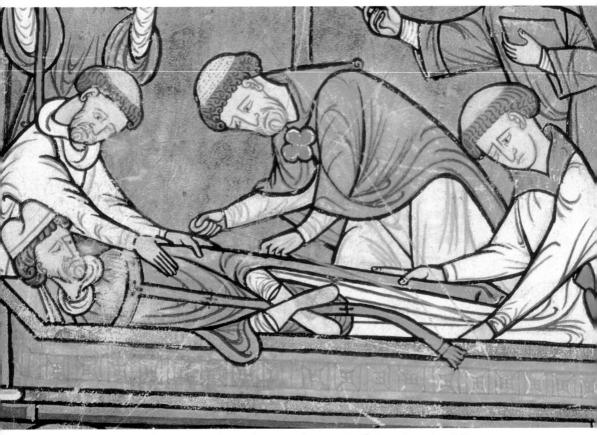

Detail of the burial of Thomas Becket in the crypt; from an English psalter of *c.* 1200.

later, on 27 September 1538, Wriothesley recounted a conversation he had had with Stephen Gardiner, Bishop of Winchester, who 'did not seem to dislike the doing at Canterbury, and wished the like were done at Winchester'.[20] The letter gave no indication of the nature of the difference between Winchester and Canterbury: it might have been that Becket's bones were burned and Swithin's were not, but that is not a necessary conclusion to be drawn from the correspondence. It may equally have been the case that Becket's relics were reinterred in an appropriate grave somewhere within the Cathedral, while those of Swithin were scattered or dispersed in some other way.

At Durham, as noted in Chapter 4, the Commissioners arrived in 1537 and opened the shrine of St Cuthbert with such force that one of the leg bones was broken; but the body (which, curiously, seems to have been preserved intact) was then left in the Cathedral revestry to await the King's decision on its disposal – during which time, according to the

116

Benedictine tradition, the monks removed it for secret burial in another part of the Cathedral.

That much the same might have happened to the remains of St William at York is revealed in a document published in 1736.[21] St William's shrine, which had stood in the nave of York Minster, was demolished by the Commissioners for York and 'no remembrance left of the place'. A tradition persisted, however, that the saint's body lay beneath a marble stone in the nave, which was raised in the course of repaving the Minster in May 1732. Beneath it was a stone coffin covered by a lid with an embossed cross – apparently very similar to the unidentified stone in the Chapel of St Mary Magdalene in the north crypt transept at Canterbury. Inside was a square, lead box containing bones. No inscriptions or other identifying features were found. The bones may or may not have been the remains of St William.

The events at Chichester, Lincoln, Winchester, Durham and York suggest that the treatment of saintly relics was left to the local Commissioners, who disposed of them in ways that would prevent them from becoming the objects of renewed superstition and veneration. No record has been found of any burning of bones at these five places. Stanley's opinion was that, in most places, the bones of the unshrined saints were buried 'with decency and care near the places where their shrines had stood'.[22] The same may have happened at Canterbury. Becket, however, was not like any other saint: he stood, as no other saint did, for an ecclesiastical theory against which both Henry and Cromwell had declared war, and the King dealt with Canterbury in a different way to the other English Cathedrals. It was, for example, the only New Foundation Cathedral at which the old prior was not allowed to become the new Dean, and the King also encouraged the foundation of the College of Six Preachers at Canterbury to teach and preach against the authority of the Pope. A proclamation from the King at Westminster in November 1538 made plain the depth of the royal displeasure against Canterbury's saint.[23] It noted that Thomas Becket, sometime Archbishop of Canterbury, was 'really a rebel who fled to France and to the bishop of Rome to procure the abrogation of wholesome laws', and it commanded that henceforth Becket

> shall no longer be named a saint . . . his pictures throughout the realm are to be plucked down and his festivals shall no longer be kept, and the services in his name shall be razed out of all books.

It would not, in the light of this, be surprising to find that Becket's remains were singled out for special treatment, and a document exists

The destruction of the images of St Thomas Becket; a screen in the church of Burlingham St Andrew, Norfolk: the painting of Becket has been scratched out completely.

among the *Letters and Papers of Henry VIII* purporting to describe just such treatment.[24] Dated 24 April 1538, it claims to be a sentence passed on Becket following a mock 'trial' conducted at his shrine at which, naturally enough, he failed to appear. The sentence was that:

> Thomas, formerly Archbishop of Canterbury, having been cited, and noone having appeared for him, judgement is given that in his lifetime he disturbed the realm, and his crimes were the cause of his death, although the people hold him for a martyr. He is therefore never to be named martyr in future, his bones are to be taken up and publicly burnt and the treasures of his shrine confiscated to the King .... This sentence pronounced, the King commanded it to be put into execution 11th August. The gold and silver of the shrine filled 26 waggons. On

118

the 19th (St Bernard's day) the sacrilege was completed and the relics publicly burnt and the ashes scattered.

As the footnote in the *Letters and Papers* points out, however, it is 'pretty certain' that this cannot have been a genuine contemporary document. It differs in important respects from the format of other official papers; the King is described as 'Rex Hiberniae', though he did not take the title until 1541 or 1542; there is no corroboration of the story in other contemporary documents or correspondence; and in any case, St Bernard's day does not fall on 19 August. Most damaging of all to the claim for authenticity is the fact that, while the document claims the bones were burned on 19 August 1538, the shrine was still in place at the end of that month: on 1 September, Sir William Pennison wrote to Thomas Cromwell about a visit that was paid to the shrine 'upon Friday last at 6' by Madame de Montreuil.[25] The letter describes in some detail the French lady's tour of the Cathedral, culminating in a visit to the shrine itself.

> Thus over looking and vewing more than an owre, as well the shryne, as Saint Thomas hed, being at both sett cousshins to knyle, and the Pryour, openyng Sainct Thomas hed, saing to her 3 tymes, 'This is Sainc Thomas Hed', and offered her to kisse it; but she nother knyled, nor would kysse it, but styll vewing the riches thereof she departed, and went to her lodging to dynner.[26]

The story that the bones of St Thomas had been burned appears to have originated on the mainland of Europe, where Catholic opinion was outraged by the King's action. At a consistory at Rome on 25 October 1538, the Pope 'announced the new cruelty and impiety of the King of England, who had commanded the body of St Thomas of Canterbury to be burnt and the ashes scattered to the wind'.[27]

A few weeks later, on 6 December 1538, Castelnau, Bishop of Tarbes, noted in a letter that 'the Pope's nuncio presses for vengeance for the relics of St Edward and St Thomas of Canterbury';[28] and later the same month (17 December) Pope Paul III promulgated a bull of excommunication against King Henry VIII that had first been prepared (but never executed) in 1535. In it, the Pope specifically accused the King of having ordered the burning of St Thomas's bones following a mock trial:

> for whereas the bones of St Thomas, Archbishop of Canterbury, because of the innumerable miracles wrought at them by Almighty God, were kept with the utmost reverence in the said realm of

England in the City of Canterbury in an ark of gold, after the King had caused the said St Thomas . . . to be summoned to a trial . . . and declared a traitor, he has commanded those bones to be exhumed and burned, and the ashes scattered to the wind.[29]

In passing, the curious use of the word 'exhumed' may be noted. It may mean nothing more than that the bones were taken out of the shrine before being burned; but the word 'exhumed' – and the original Latin word *exhumari* – usually suggests the removal of a body or bones from the earth. The hint in the bull that the bones of Becket may have been buried somewhere else before being burned is of interest in the light of the hypotheses discussed in the next chapter.

Interest in the fate of Becket's bones spread quickly throughout Europe. In October 1538, only a month after the destruction of the shrine, Thomas Knight, who was on an official mission to the Court of Brussels, sent a letter to Thomas Cromwell from Valenciennes, in northern France. 'Every man who seeks news from England,' he wrote, 'enquires what has become of the Saint of Canterbury.'[30] The answer he gave was tantalising: that Thomas Wriothesley, the first Earl of Southampton, who had actually been present at the destruction of the shrine in Canterbury and whom he was accompanying on the mission to Brussels, 'had sufficiently instructed me to answer such questions'. Regrettably, there is no record of the substance of Wriothesley's instruction.

In the following month (November 1538) a note sent by Sir Thomas Wyatt to Mr Philip Hoby, a returning ambassador to Spain, referred to 'the burning of the saint's bones';[31] and early in 1539 Wyatt wrote to Cromwell from Toledo wishing he could 'persuade the preachers to preach his Grace's grave proceedings against sacramentaries and anabaptists as they do the burning of the bishop's [Becket's] bones'.[32]

Whether justified or not, the belief seems rapidly to have gained ground in Catholic Europe, accompanied by an appropriate sense of indignation, that the remains of saints had been consumed by fire. Writing to the King from Brussels in November 1538, Thomas Wriothesley and others reported a recent supper-party they had attended with the Marquis of Barrow, who 'said it was thought in these parts that all religion was extinct in England, that we had no mass, that the saints were burnt, and all that was holy subverted'.[33] A letter written to the Emperor Charles V by Reginald Pole (later to become the last Roman Catholic Archbishop of Canterbury in the reign of Mary Tudor) in February 1539 continued to fan the flames of righteous Catholic indignation over the King's alleged action.[34]

Tho: Wiatt Knight.

Sir Thomas Wyatt by Hans Holbein.

Thou hast heard what proofs of ungodliness Henry has exhibited upon the tomb and body of St Thomas. Thou hast heard of this first kind of sacrilege, how he plundered and despoiled the shrine which was studded with so many offerings of kings, princes and peoples .... But that afterwards he should pluck from it the bones of a man who had died so many centuries before him, should cast them into the fire, and when they were reduced to ashes should then scatter them in despite to the wind, has anyone ever read of such an example of barbarity?

It is interesting that the same phrase 'scattered to the wind' occurs in many of these written accounts, suggesting that they derived either from each other or from one common source or legend. The source appears to be the record of the consistory at Rome in October 1538, in which the phrase first appeared. What may have been passed on, therefore, was the papal interpretation of the events in Canterbury, which, as noted above, had no independent corroboration in contemporary English documents. The vivid imagery of ashes being scattered to the wind may not have originated with, or been confined to, the supposed fate of Becket's bones. In March 1539 Reginald Pole, in a letter to the Constable of France, wrote of 'the enemies of God raged against his saints . . . whose most sacred bodies have been infamously torn from the tomb, burnt, and their ashes scattered to the wind'.[35] Such distinctive wording may simply have been used as a standard formula to condemn the general actions of the King in disposing of saintly relics.

In time, the accusations of the Pope and of Reginald Pole came to be repeated in a number of other Catholic publications. These included works by Thomas Stapleton, a prebendary of Chichester under Mary Tudor and one of the most learned Catholics of his day, and by Nicholas Sanders, a Catholic theologian who took refuge on the continent and who there wrote a critique of the religious life of England under Elizabeth.[36] Father Robert Parsons (or Persons), a Jesuit priest who converted to Catholicism in 1575 after an academic career in which he had been 'a most learned and zealous opponent of popery', quoted extensively from the papal bull in confirmation of the indignities perpetrated against St Thomas, but he had no other evidence to support the claim for the burning of the saint's bones.[37]

A further testimony to the burning is claimed to have been given by Nycander Nucius, a wandering Greek. The story was recounted by William Urry in his unpublished biography of Becket.[38] Urry claimed that the story had been in print since 1841, though regrettably his manuscript failed to identify its source. According to the story, Nucius attached himself to a German ambassadorial party that arrived in England in 1545 and passed through Canterbury on its way to London. Despite the obvious barrier of language, Nucius managed to glean several pieces of recent news, including the destruction of St Thomas's shrine and the burning of the bones in the midst of the city. Then, he said, the ashes were forthwith put into a cannon and fired into the air. 'It is easy to reject the story,' Urry observed, 'but could it not be true? Present at the time was Thomas Cromwell, the ex-soldier, and this is just what might be expected of his grim sense of humour.'

A sixteenth-century document that has probably caused more trouble than it is worth is Nicholas Harpsfield's *The Life and Death of Sr Thomas More*. As noted in Chapter 3, it was this work (or rather, a false quotation from it) that led to so much confusion in the flurry of correspondence following the discovery of the coffin in the eastern crypt in 1888. Harpsfield, sometime Professor of Greek at Oxford, was Archdeacon of Canterbury during Mary Tudor's brief reign between 1553 and 1558, where he was zealous in the Catholic cause. He was committed to the Tower of London in 1563, probably on a charge of seditious and disorderly conduct, where he died in 1583.[39] His *Life and Death of Sr Thomas More* remained in manuscript form until its eventual publication in 1932.[40] In the years prior to 1920, when Mason was preparing his own book on the fate of Becket's bones, at least two of Harpsfield's unpublished manuscripts existed, one in the British Museum and one in Lambeth Palace. In the version that Mason consulted, Harpsfield wrote, in a passage that commended the similarities between the martyrdoms of Thomas More and Thomas Becket:

> Albeit we have of late (God illuminate our beetle blind hearts to see and repent our folly and impiety!) unshrined him [Becket] and burned his holy bones, and not only unshrined and unsainted him, but have made him also (after so many hundred years) a traitor to the king that honoured him.[41]

This statement is probably of limited value: Harpsfield was not in Canterbury at the time of the destruction of the shrine, having arrived for the first time as Archdeacon in 1554, so he had no first-hand knowledge of the events that took place in September 1538. In writing that the bones were burned, he may simply have been following the views that had been promoted by the Pope and Reginald Pole.[42] On the other hand he would, as Archdeacon during the Catholic restoration, almost certainly have known about the burial of the bones, if that is what had really happened to them; and it would then have been curious for him to have persisted with the story of the burning.

The confusion over Harpsfield's text sprang from Christopher Wordsworth's *Ecclesiastical Biography*, the second edition of which was published in 1818.[43] In it, Wordsworth included the text of a *Life of Sir Thomas More* which he had transcribed from a collection of manuscripts then residing in the Lambeth Palace Library. The author of the *Life* was unknown: the preface to the work was signed simply by one calling himself Ro:Ba. Nevertheless, Wordsworth went to some trouble, in introducing the text, to ascribe the authorship to Harpsfield.[44] He based this ascription partly on the fact that Harpsfield was known to have written a biography of More, and partly on the fact that Ro:Ba declared in his preface that he was also writing a special work on the divorce of Henry VIII and Queen Catherine of Aragon – which Harpsfield later did. Unsurprisingly, those who had failed to consult one of the original manuscripts of Harpsfield's *Life and Death of Sr Thomas More* simply followed Wordsworth in assuming that the text published in the 1818 edition of *Ecclesiastical Biography* was that of Harpsfield himself.

For much of the text, the confusion over its real authorship is probably of little significance. Whole passages are identical between Harpsfield's work and the work reproduced by Wordsworth. Plainly, whoever Ro:Ba was, he was quite content to copy out, almost verbatim, the text of Harpsfield's biography of More. Indeed, he humbly confessed as much in his preface (which, crucially, Wordsworth failed to include in the 1818 edition of *Ecclesiastical Biography*).

> The most part of this booke is none of my owne; I onely challenge the ordering and translating. The most of the rest is Stapleton's and Harpsfield's, so patronaged under the wings of theire fame I may the more boldly presse into the viewe of the world. Gentle reader, by thy severe censure, discourage not a young beginner. Yor servant in our Lo:Jesus. Ro:Ba.[45]

With respect to the critical sentence about the relics of St Thomas, however, Ro:Ba made a vital change to Harpsfield's text. Whereas Harpsfield clearly wrote that 'we have unshrined him and *burned* his holy bones',[46] Ro:Ba wrote: 'Albeit we have of late (God give us the grace to repent, and see our folie and impietie!) unshrined him and *buried* his holie relicks'.[47]

To those who, mistakenly, believed these words to be those of Harpsfield himself, their significance was indeed startling: here was the Catholic Archdeacon of Canterbury, writing only some twenty years after the destruction of the shrine of St Thomas, asserting, in flat contradiction to the orthodox view, that the bones had not been burned after all, but buried. Without knowing the identity of Ro:Ba the significance of his mistranscription from Harpsfield cannot be assessed. It may simply have been a clerical error, but it may also be the case that Ro:Ba had knowledge that Harpsfield lacked.

That it may *not* have been a simple clerical error is suggested by the fact that the variation between the two pieces of text is not confined to this one word. A comparison between the two texts shows that Ro:Ba also made other changes within the shell of Harpsfield's sentence: for example, he omitted Harpsfield's graphic phrase about 'our beetle blind hearts', and he wrote of 'holie relicks' rather than 'holy bones'. It would appear that Ro:Ba was acting deliberately rather than accidentally in changing Harpsfield's text, and he clearly wished to say that Becket's relics had been buried. If, as Wordsworth thought likely, Ro:Ba was writing towards the end of Queen Elizabeth's reign,[48] then his work must have post-dated that of Harpsfield by several years, and may well have been based on information that was not available to Harpsfield. Ro:Ba must, however tentatively, be regarded as a witness for the burial of Becket's bones, not their burning.

The story of the burning gained ground in England through the writings of the sixteenth-century chroniclers, especially Wriothesley, Stow and Holinshed. Charles Wriothesley, who was born in 1508, was a first cousin of Thomas Wriothesley (later to become the first Earl of Southampton) who was one of the Commissioners for the destruction of the shrine of St Thomas at Canterbury. There is no evidence that Charles himself was present in Canterbury in 1538, though two of the authors cited in Chapter 4 (Beazeley and Pollen) suggested that Commissioner Wriothesley and chronicler Wriothesley were one and the same person. Mason was of the opinion that there was little intimacy between the two cousins.[49] It is possible that Charles Wriothesley did not have access to any special information that would not have been equally available to most other well-informed Englishmen of his day. He may, in other words, have been retailing the conventional wisdom of the time rather than making an authoritative statement of what was done. But his account of the events in 1538 was quite unambiguous.[50]

Allso Saint Austen's [i.e. Augustine's] Abbey, at Canterbury, was suppressed, and the shryne and goodes taken to the Kinges treasurye, and St Thomas of Canterburies shryne allso, and the monks commaunded to chaunge their habettes, and then after they should knowe the Kinges further pleasure; and the bones of St Thomas of Canterbury were brent [i.e. burnt] in the same church by my Lord Crumwell.

That much is clear enough: the bones were burnt in the church by the Lord Privy Seal, Thomas Cromwell. Wriothesley's account continues, however, with a statement that appears at first sight to be rather strange, though in fact it opens up an interesting possibility:

They found his head hole with the bones, which had a wounde in the skull, for the monkes had closed another skull in silver richly, for people to offer to, which they sayd was St Thomas skull, so that nowe the abuse was openly knowne that they had used many yeres afore.[51]

The first part presents no difficulties: among the bones that were removed from the shrine was the saint's skull, complete with the wounds of his martyrdom. This is no more than would be expected from the accounts of the translation in 1220 (see Chapter 1), for although those accounts agree that a number of small bones were kept out of the shrine for distribution to the great and the good, there is not the slightest hint that these included anything as large as the skull. The skull, then, was in the shrine from 1220 to 1538. Yet something that purported to be the skull of St Thomas was shown to pilgrims visiting the Cathedral and given to them to kiss. Erasmus described how, during his and John Colet's visit to the crypt in about 1512, they were shown the 'perforated skull of the martyr ... covered in silver, but the forehead is left bare for people to kiss'.[52] Likewise Madame de Montreuil, visiting the Cathedral a week or so before the destruction of the shrine, was shown 'St Thomas hed' which was 'offered her to kysse it'.[53] It appears, then, from Wriothesley's record, that a faked skull, encased in a silver reliquary, had been used for many years to fool the pilgrims, doubtless with the intention of extracting as much money as possible. With the removal of Becket's bones from the shrine, skull and all, the abuse became openly known.

John Stow, chronicler and antiquarian, was younger than Wriothesley, having been born in about 1525 (*Dictionary of National Biography*). He was only thirteen years old when the shrine of St Thomas was destroyed, and could scarcely have had first-hand knowledge of it. From 1560 onwards he devoted himself to the collection of books, documents, charters and manuscripts about English history, archaeology and literature. Among them may have been Wriothesley's *Chronicle*, for there is an obvious linguistic similarity between his account and Stow's. The 1592 edition of Stow's *Annals* described the events at Canterbury in 1538 thus:

> St Augustines abbey at Canterbury was suppressed, and the shrine and goods taken to the King's treasurie, as also the shrine of Thomas Beckett in the priorie of Christ Church, was likewise taken to the Kings use. The shrine was builded about a mans height, all of stone, then upwarde of tymber plain, within ye which was a Chest of yron, conteining the bones of Thomas Becket, scul and al, with the wounde of his death and the peece cut out of his scull layde in the same wounde. These bones (by commaundement of the L. Cromwell) were then and there brent.[54]

Holinshed's *Chronicle*, printed in 1586, adds little to those of the others since it uses almost identical language to describe the fate of Becket's bones. He must have drawn his material from either Wriothesley or Stow, or from an independent source common to the three of them. He writes of the skull being found with the bones, of the piece broken out of the skull by the wound of Becket's death, and of the burning in the church by Lord Cromwell. What is interesting about each of these three statements is that, although they all use similar language to describe the destruction of the bones, they seem to have derived from a source other than the record of the consistory at Rome in October 1538. The stories circulating on the continent all stressed that, the bones having been burned, the ashes were scattered to the winds; but no such vivid detail appears in the English chronicles. Instead, they dwell upon the finding of the skull in the shrine, and, in Wriothesley's *Chronicle*, upon the consequent exposure of the fraud perpetrated by the monks.

The disposal of saintly bones and the destruction of their shrines upset a great many English subjects. Becket's fate, in particular, was seen as an outrage: it was deeply deplored and angrily resented both by those who were consciously opposed to the new ecclesiastical policy and also by those who looked upon the Canterbury pilgrimages as a valuable source of amusement and profit. Feelings ran so high that, for reasons of what would now be called 'public relations' or 'policy presentation', an account of the policy had to be given to the people. It was done in the form of a statement drawn up at the end of 1538 or the beginning of 1539, entitled *Official Account of the Reformation. Vindication of the Changes Recently Effected in England.*[55]

The authorship of the statement is unknown, but the extant draft is in the hand of Thomas Derby, who was the clerk of the Privy Council for a number of years including 1539. Milman and others surmised that, since the document was headed by a text (from the First Epistle of Peter), it may have been intended as a sermon to be preached from St Paul's cross or elsewhere. Alternatively, it may simply have been intended for use on the continent by ambassadors and agents who wished to promote the King's point of view. At all events, the document seems to be some sort of official reply to the charges of Rome. Its reference to the fate of St Thomas's shrine is of great interest. It begins with the words 'as to the shrine of Thos Becket . . . ', and continues with a reconstructed history of Becket's crimes against the royal prerogative. There then appears the following text.

> His [Becket's] shrine and bones are therefore taken away and bestowed where they will cause no superstition afterwards.

There is no intimation here of any burning; the phrase 'taken away and bestowed' implies exactly the reverse. The sentence then continues:

> as it is indeed amongst others of that sorte conveyed and buried in a noble tower.

127

This part of the sentence has been crossed through, as though being deleted from the draft version either by the instruction of the Privy Council or merely as a change of mind by the writer. Yet the phrase has been regarded as being of some significance in suggesting that the bones of Becket were indeed buried, and in a 'noble tower'. The identity of the mysterious tower can only be guessed at. Milman took it to mean the corona, or tower at the eastern end of the Trinity Chapel in Canterbury Cathedral (see Chapter 2), although this appears to be a rather fanciful suggestion, scarcely moderated by his additional surmise about the motive of Cardinal Pole in wishing to be buried there.[56] Mason, by contrast, took the view that the tower in question was the Tower of London, to which the jewels and metals from the shrine were probably taken. In other known cases, such as that of St Richard at Chichester, the Commission required the relics of the unshrined saint (including his bones) to be taken to the Tower of London along with the treasure; and Mason surmised that whoever wrote the first draft of this statement had made the same assumption about the relics of St Thomas at Canterbury, only to be corrected later when it became apparent that they had actually been buried elsewhere.[57]

The text of the statement did not end there; it continued:

> And foreasmuch as his head almost whole was found with the rest of the bones closed within the shrine, and there was in that church a great skull of another head, but much greater by three quarter parts than that part which was lacking in the head closed within the shrine, whereby it appeared that the same was but a feigned fiction; if this head was burnt, was therefore St Thomas's burnt? Assuredly, it concludeth not.

The first part of this confirms the observations of Wriothesley, Stow and Holinshed that the bones removed from the shrine included the skull of Becket, though it appears to contradict them in asserting that part of the skull was missing (or, at least, appeared to be missing). It also confirms Wriothesley's charge against the monks that, for a long time, they had deceived the pilgrims by showing them a skull that was falsely claimed to be that of Becket – a 'great skull of another head' that was nothing more than a 'feigned fiction'. The text is careful to observe that this second, faked skull could not have been the part that was missing from the real skull, for it was much larger than the missing part.

The implication in the next clause of the passage is that it was the faked skull that was burned, not the skull removed from the shrine, leading the writer to pose the rhetorical question: if this (faked) head was burned, were the bones of St Thomas burned? The answer the writer gives to his own question is tantalising: 'assuredly not'. The impression created by this answer upon a cursory reading of the text is that the bones of Becket were not burned; but the text does not allow this interpretation. That the faked skull was burned is not itself sufficient evidence to permit the conclusion that Becket's skull and bones were not. The writer appears to have gone to some lengths to create the impression that no such burning took place, yet without explicitly saying so. His admission about the burning of the faked skull, however, does suggest that something was burned; and this might, of course, have been the action giving rise to the stories of burning in the first place.

The final sentence of the statement could be regarded in a similar way:

> St Swithun and other reliques, whereabout abuse of hypocrisy was, are laid safe, and not as it is untruly surmitted burnt. They are put away secretly, as some say the body of Moses was hidden lest the Jews should fall to idolatory.

The text affirms that, in the case of St Swithin at Winchester, a similar charge of burning was made which in fact was false: the bones were secretly 'laid safe' in a place where they could give rise to no superstition. The inclusion of this text immediately following the case of St Thomas may well have been intended to convey the impression of innocence by association: if St Swithin's bones were not burned, in spite of rumours to the contrary, then neither were St Thomas's. But the conclusion does not follow the premiss; and the fact remains that this piece of text, of which a great deal has been made in the literature, does not explicitly declare that no burning took place. It does, however, clearly state that Becket's bones were taken away and bestowed in a place that would not later give rise to any superstition; and this, by reasonable implication, precludes their destruction by fire.

Both Mason and Milman relied quite heavily upon this 1539 document to support their conclusion that Becket's bones had not been burned; but others have disagreed. In particular, Beazeley, in his 1913 pamphlet *The Canterbury Bones*, not only dismissed its attempted defence of the King's action as an outright lie, but also suggested that Milman's interpretation of the passage had been a false one.[58] Beazeley was quite clear that the burning had indeed occurred, and he explained the deleted clause about the removal of the bones to a 'noble tower' as false testimony that even the writer of the document could not eventually bring himself to include:

'Even the very elastic consciences of Tudor days could not stand such a flagrant terminological inexactitude.'

A further defence of the King's actions was made by one of Thomas Derby's successors as clerk of the Privy Council, William Thomas. Thomas, a man of learning who was at one time a member of the King's embassy at Venice, published a dialogue in 1552 (*Il Pellegrino Inglese*) in which an English pilgrim discourses with some Italian gentlemen about the King's behaviour. The piece was published first in Italian and later, in 1774 and again in 1861, in English. Several copies exist in England: the version reproduced by Mason was that kept in the British Museum.

In the dialogue, the English pilgrim is asked:

> The poore St Thomas of Canterburye, alas it sufficed hym [that is, the King] not just to spoyle and devour the great ryches of his shryne, whos treasure amounted to so manye thousand crownes; but to be avenged on the dead corpse dyd he not cause his bones openly to be burned?[59]

In reply, the pilgrim concedes the great amount of wealth that the King appropriated from the shrine at the time of its destruction, but goes on to recite a long litany of the superstitious and deceitful things perpetrated by the monks at Canterbury, including a claim that the blood-coloured water from a freshwater spring, which the monks themselves had doctored with red ochre, was the blood of the holy martyr, capable of miraculous cures. The pilgrim continues:

> The kyng . . . could no lesse do then deface the shryne that was the Auther of so muche ydolatry. Whether the doyng thereof hath bene the undoyng of the canonised saint or not, I cannot tell. Butt this is true, that the bones are spred amongest the bones of so many dead men, that without some greate Miracle they wyll not be founde agayne.[60]

(In the manuscripts in the Bodleian Library and Lambeth Palace, the phrase 'the bones' is replaced by 'his bones'.) As noted in Chapter 4, it was this testimony that helped to persuade Milman in 1891, and later Routledge in 1895, of the continuing existence of the bones. Mason, too, was evidently impressed by it. 'It may be doubted,' he wrote, 'whether William Thomas had a first-hand and independent knowledge of the facts; but he had been trained in the traditions of Cromwell and was steeped in the official atmosphere of Henry's reign, and his virtual denial of the burning of the bones has more than ordinary significance.'[61]

What, then, is to be made of this assorted and conflicting evidence? There appear to be five main strands: the absence of any direct, contemporary evidence that the Canterbury Commissioners burned the bones that were removed from the shrine of St Thomas; the tradition begun at the consistory in Rome in October 1538 and widely repeated throughout continental Europe that the bones had been burned and the ashes scattered to the winds; the tradition in the English chronicles that the bones had been removed, skull and all, and burned in the Cathedral by Cromwell; the tradition that a fake skull had been burned as well as, or instead of, the real relics; and the publicity favourable to the King, corroborated by the anonymous Ro:Ba, which insisted that the bones had been buried somewhere.

It would be difficult, in view of the obvious conflict of evidence and the apparent absence of any incontestable grounds for preferring one strand over the others, to assert with absolute confidence that the bones of Becket either were or were not burned by the Commissioners in 1538. The evidence, if taken selectively, could be used to support a number of possible reconstructions of the events that took place.

First, and most obviously, the real relics may indeed have been burned by Thomas Cromwell and the ashes scattered in the winds, as claimed in the stories originating at the Roman consistory and taken up by the English chroniclers.

Secondly, the real relics may have been buried in a discreet and unmarked grave by the Commissioners, acting in collaboration with the Priory of Christ Church. This appears to have happened to the remains of unshrined saints elsewhere, and the treatment accorded to St Thomas of Canterbury may have been no different. It is certain that some of the monks and chief officers of the priory were paid by the Commissioners for their assistance in 'the disgarnishing of a shrine and other things there'.[62] Quite separately, the faked skull and other dubious relics may have been burned, thus giving rise to the popular belief that bones were burned at Canterbury and the ashes scattered.

Thirdly, the monks may have secretly removed the relics from the shrine some time before the arrival of the Commissioners, buried them in another place, and substituted other bones in the shrine for the Commissioners to find. If the monks' deception had succeeded and the spurious bones been burned by the Commissioners, this alone would have given rise to the obviously well-founded belief about the burning. Although this possibility has been suggested in the literature,[63] there are no direct parallels for such action elsewhere.

It is quite credible that the monks were capable of some act of this sort. Bones and other relics were frequently moved from place to place for all manner of reasons.[64] Their predecessors, shortly after the martyrdom, had had no qualms about removing Becket's body from its marble coffin in the crypt and hiding it in a wooden chest behind the altar of Our Lady in the Undercroft (see Chapter 1). Similarly the monks at Durham had, according to a Benedictine tradition, swapped the body of St Cuthbert for that of a monk exhumed from the cemetery outside; but this was carried out after the arrival of the Commissioners, not before, while the King was apparently deciding what to do with the saint's remains (Chapter 4). Obvious though it may seem that the monks at Canterbury must have tried very hard to do whatever they could to protect the precious relics from destruction by the Commissioners, there is no hint in the contemporary documents of any such anticipatory behaviour on their part. The reason may lie in their fear of what would have happened to them if their deception were to be discovered; or it may lie in the fact that, if they had no grounds for believing that the Commissioners would burn the bones, there was no real need to conceal them.

It is of no help, in arriving at a judgement on the evidence, that previous writers, having reviewed much the same bundle of materials, have come to sharply differing conclusions. It was seen in Chapter 4 that, of those writing between 1888 and 1920, Morris, Sheppard, Venables, Arkasden and Beazeley all held the firm view that Becket's bones had been burned. Of these, the opinion of Father John Morris deserves particular respect, since although he made some remarkable mistakes (such as his assertion that the true skull of Becket had never been placed in the shrine), he probably devoted a greater amount of care and attention to the evidence than the others. Beazeley's views, moreover, cannot be lightly dismissed, since he was at the time honorary librarian to the Dean and Chapter; nor can those of Sheppard, who was Seneschal of Canterbury.

To these names must be added the later one of Dr William Urry, who probably knew as much about Becket as any of his predecessors in the Cathedral Library and Archives. He was present at the reopening of the grave in the eastern crypt in 1949, and his views must be regarded as authoritative. In a paper on the resting places of Becket, published in 1973, Urry expressed the clear opinion that 'with King Henry VIII so close, and Cromwell evidently in the Cathedral itself, there can be little question that the saint's bones were burned.'[65]

Against these, however, can be ranged the names of Austin, Routledge, Thornton, Milman, Moore and Mason, all of whom believed that the bones had been buried rather than burned. Again, the views of most of these writers deserve to be respected. Routledge had been a member of the original Investigating Committee; Milman was Director of the Society of Antiquaries; Moore was an internationally respected scholar and historian; and Mason had delved more deeply into the minutiae of the evidence than anyone on either side of the divide.

The position of the Dean and Chapter in 1948 adds weight to the argument in favour of a burial, for having had a great deal of time to ponder the evidence and arguments, they plainly decided that Becket's bones had not been burned, but were residing in the coffin in the eastern crypt. It may perhaps be thought that they had much to lose from a false judgement in the matter, for they would have had to endure an unwelcome degree of embarrassment had they entombed some bones that might simply have been those of an anonymous old man. The fact that wise counsels may have prevailed at the eleventh hour to save them from the risk of such embarrassment does not affect their judgement on the issue of the burning, for the Cave report refuted the bones as those of Becket on grounds *other than* that the real bones had been burned. If the Dean and Chapter really believed in 1948 that the bones had been buried, then nothing appears to have emerged in the interim that would compel them to change their minds.

It seems, then, that it is not possible to state with absolute certainty that the bones of St Thomas Becket either were or were not burned in 1538. People may reasonably differ, and have differed, in their assessments of the evidence. Many have held firmly to the view that the evidence permits no other conclusion than that the bones of St Thomas were burned by Cromwell's Commissioners in 1538. Others have been led to the contrary opinion that they were more likely to have been buried. For the former, there are no further questions to be addressed: the bones were burned, and that is an end of the matter. For the latter, the question remains: if Becket's relics were *not* burned in 1538, what did happen to them? And is their fate in some way linked to the mysterious grave in the eastern crypt that was first opened in 1888?

Murder of Thomas Becket, from the Luttrell Psalter, English, *c.* 1340.

8   *Five Hypotheses*

The relics of Thomas Becket may or may not have been burned when his shrine was destroyed in 1538. If they were not burned, they may have been taken secretly by the monks and buried without the knowledge or consent of the King's Commissioners, or they may have been buried in an inconspicuous place by the Commissioners, probably acting in collaboration with the monks and officers of the priory. The evidence appears to be insufficiently conclusive to permit an incontestable opinion. In addressing the question of the identity of the skeleton exhumed in 1888, allowance must consequently be made for the fact that the grave site may or may not be associated in some way with one of three possible treatments accorded to Becket's relics in 1538. In pulling the evidence together, this chapter can deal in nothing more than hypotheses, judging a number of alternatives in the light of the available evidence. Logically, the alternatives can be set out in the following way:

Fate of Becket's relics in 1538	Connection between the '1888 grave site' and Becket?	
	No	*Yes*
Burned	Hypothesis 1	–
Buried secretly by the monks	Hypothesis 2	Hypothesis 4
Buried by Commissioners in collaboration with the monks	Hypothesis 3	Hypothesis 5

Hypothesis 1: that Becket's bones were burned in 1538, and that there is no connection between Becket and the '1888 grave site'

The first hypothesis assumes that Becket's bones were burned in 1538, and that they cannot be connected with the grave discovered in the

View of the Trinity Chapel from the east end
showing the position of Cardinal Châtillon's tomb
in relation to the site of Becket's shrine.

eastern crypt in 1888. The identity of the skeleton thus becomes a matter of investigation in its own right, to be considered on its own internal evidence. From this point of view, several suggestions have been made about the man whose skeleton it was, some of which have already been encountered.

It had been Beazeley's proposition in 1913, in his pamphlet *The Canterbury Bones*, that the skeleton was that of the Abbot of Evesham, William de Audeville, who may have been buried in that place in 1159.[1] It was clear even in Beazeley's day, however, that such a proposition was untenable: it is difficult to imagine the circumstances in which the Abbot's remains, having doubtless first been buried in a coffin with all the vestments and trappings that would accompany a man of his stature, would have been crudely resurrected and reburied in an ill-suited coffin in a shallow grave without accompanying vestments or regalia. The findings reported by Professor Cave in 1951 merely underscored the improbability of Beazeley's proposition, for the further, equally unlikely assumption would have to be made that the Abbot's body had also been buried coffin-less in the earth for a period of time. It is perhaps unfortunate that the Portland stone coffin was not raised and the ground beneath it explored either in 1888 or in 1949. Had that been done, the coffin of William de Audeville might perhaps have been uncovered and the issue resolved beyond dispute.

A second suggestion is that the skeleton may have been that of another saint or, at least, an eminent cleric. Mason, for example, cited the conjecture of his brother that if the bones were not Becket's, then they might have been those of St Alphege.[2] Alphege, who was Archbishop of Canterbury in the early years of the eleventh century, was captured by Viking invaders in 1011 and cruelly treated by them before being murdered at Greenwich some seven months later.[3] His body was placed in St Paul's church in London for eleven years before being returned to Canterbury, where his relics were enshrined on the north side of the high altar in the presence of King Canute. The relics survived the great fire of 1174 and were reinstated in the same position, to the north of the high altar, in William the Englishman's new choir.[4] Their fate at the time of the Reformation, when all the shrines were destroyed, is uncertain, though some believe that they were undisturbed and are still interred beside the high altar. It is improbable, however, that the skeleton in the eastern crypt could be that of Alphege. It is unlikely that he would have escaped skeletal injury at the hands of the Vikings (indeed, there is a tradition that he was killed by an axe-blow to the head), and there is nothing to suggest that his body was ever consigned to an earth burial in a common burial place.

St Alphege is captured by the Danes; from the 13th-century stained glass window in the north choir aisle triforium.

The latter objection might also be raised against other saints whose names could be associated with the skeleton, most notably St Wilfrid and St Odo, and many lesser-known archbishops whose remains were enshrined or entombed in the cathedral on the eve of the Reformation: Wulfhelm, Aethelgar, Siric, Aelfric, Bregwyn and Aethelm.[5] To attribute the skeleton to any of them would require the improbable assumption that, prior to the enshrinement or entombment of their relics, their corpses had been buried, coffin-less, in earth and subsequently exhumed with (to quote Professor Cave) 'gross and destructive carelessness'.

A third suggestion, which can probably be dispatched as speedily as the second, is that the bones were those of an ancient person, possibly even from pre-Christian times, who had originally been buried in what is now that area of the crypt, and whose remains had been carelessly dug up by those who were building or altering that part of the Cathedral. This is most likely to have happened during the building of the eastern crypt between 1179 and 1181, when part of the ancient graveyard at that end of the Cathedral precincts was disturbed and some bones reburied in a trench between the crypt and the priory infirmary.[6] It would, however, require the unlikely supposition that this was the only skeleton treated in this distinctive way. If there had been any doubt about the Christian nature of the original burial, the reinterment would not have taken place in consecrated ground at all, and certainly not on the east–west axis.

A fourth, and perhaps the most plausible, suggestion about the true identity of the skeleton (assuming, for the purposes of this first hypothesis, that it is unconnected with Becket) is that it belonged to an erstwhile monk or servant of the Priory of Christ Church who had been buried in the monks' cemetery that lay to the east and south–east of the Cathedral, and whose remains had accidentally been disturbed during building or landscaping work. It is believed that such work occurred in about 1860, when superfluous canonical houses and their gardens were demolished, and human remains were said to have been brought into the crypt for reburial.[7] Such a sequence of events would account for the skeleton's original burial as a corpse, and possibly also for the extraneous earth and debris that accompanied its reinterment in the makeshift coffin in the crypt. It does, however, require the assumption that the initial burial had taken place either directly in the earth or in a wooden coffin that had rotted and exposed the corpse to the earth.

Yet the theory of the anonymous monk raises questions to which no obvious answers seem to exist. Why, even if the first spade-cut that exposed the body in the cemetery caused accidental damage to one part of the skeleton, did the exhumation continue with such apparent carelessness as to cause further extensive damage to several other parts? Why was this particular skeleton buried on the east-west axis in the central aisle of the eastern crypt when the others were, according to information that Morris had been given, buried on the north-south axis in more peripheral places?[8] Why was the reinterment in the crypt carried out so hastily that surrounding earth and debris found its way into the coffin along with some (but not all) of the bones? Why, if it was intended to be the final resting place of the anonymous monk, was the coffin buried only three or four inches beneath the surface? Why did the burial take place in a vessel that was ill-suited for its intended use as a permanent coffin? Why, if the interment had really taken place only twenty years or so before the discovery of the coffin in 1888, was there no record of its location? Above all, why, if the skeleton had indeed belonged to an anonymous monk, did the reinterment take place in this special site so intimately associated with St Thomas Becket?

It is perhaps instructive in this context that Father John Morris, the Jesuit priest who had spearheaded the assault on the Becket hypothesis in *The Times* in February and March 1888, thought at first that the skeleton was indeed that of a monk whose coffin had been transferred to the crypt when disturbed in the monks' cemetery earlier in the century (see Chapter 3). The same view had apparently been taken by Morris's fellow-sceptic, Dr Sheppard.[9] Yet Morris was forced to concede the improbability of this explanation, partly on the ground that the coffin could not have been one in which any monk had originally been buried, and partly because, in contrast to the coffins of other monks brought in from the cemetery and reburied in less prominent places in the crypt, this vessel lay east to west in its very centre, next to the former site of Becket's tomb. Morris eventually accepted that the spot was one of 'great traditional sanctity' and felt that the bones were 'the relics of some distinguished person'.[10]

There is, of course, much to commend this first hypothesis. It is relatively simple and straightforward, avoiding the awkward complexities of subterfuge and substitution that crop up in later ones. It requires no elaborate refutation of the conventional view that Becket's bones had been burned in 1538, and it might explain some of the unusual features of the skeleton described in Professor Cave's report. But the hypothesis fails to provide a convincing identity for the bones. The most commonly mentioned candidate is an anonymous monk whose rest in the neighbouring monks' cemetery had been rudely disturbed by building operations, and whose remains had been taken into the crypt for a decent reburial. This proposition fails to account for the haste and furtiveness with which the skeleton had been buried, the obviously makeshift and temporary nature of the coffin, and the special significance of the place in which it was found. None of these features would be expected to attend the reinterment of a monk (or, indeed, of anyone else) whose body had been accidentally uncovered in a cemetery.

Hypothesis 2: that Becket's bones were buried secretly by the monks in 1538, and that there is no connection between Becket and the '1888 grave site'

The second hypothesis, like the first, denies any connection between Becket and the skeleton in the eastern crypt. It therefore raises exactly the same questions about the identity of the bones as the first, and encounters exactly the same difficulties that attend any attempt to answer them. Unlike the first hypothesis, however, it asserts that Becket's bones were not burned in 1538, but were taken secretly from the shrine by the monks and interred in a place that has never become widely

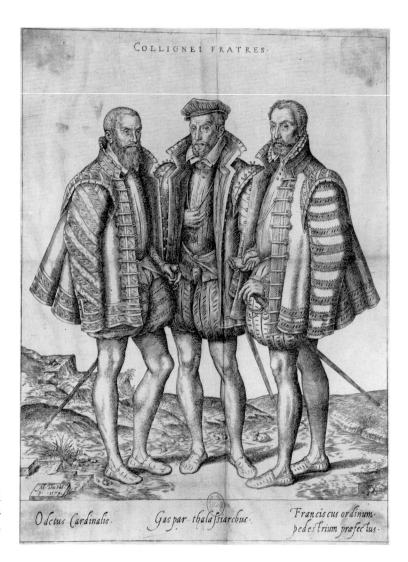

Odetus Cardinalis. *Gaspar thalassiarchus.* *Franciscus ordinum pedestrium præfectus.*

Odet de Coligny (Cardinal
Châtillon), left, and his
brothers, by Martin Du Val,
1579.

known. The particular question raised by this hypothesis is: where might the burial have taken place, and is that place accessible today? Of course the bones may, on this hypothesis, have been taken beyond the Cathedral precincts or even beyond the city of Canterbury for interment; but it is beyond the scope of this book to explore such legends. This chapter confines itself to possible sites within or surrounding the Cathedral, a number of which suggest themselves for consideration on the basis of the evidence reviewed so far.

It was the reported contention of Peregrine Prescott, the young man who was apprehended in the Cathedral precincts in 1990, that the saint's

140

remains had finally been deposited in the tomb of Cardinal Châtillon (Odet de Coligny), in the Trinity Chapel (see the Prologue). Such a claim appears to have been made by no one else, and there seems to be no other evidence to support it. An extraordinary sequence of events would be required to explain it, since Coligny did not die until 1571, thirty-three years after the destruction of the shrine. Nevertheless, there are some obvious peculiarities about his tomb.

Its location in the Trinity Chapel, cutting into one of the abutting pillars and as close as any other tomb to the hallowed site of Becket's shrine, is not an obvious place in which to leave a coffin for a short period of time, pending the repatriation of the body to France. The only other tombs in this part of the Trinity Chapel are those of distinctly more eminent people who were gradually allowed to breach the rule that nothing other than the shrine of the saint should be permitted to stand in the Chapel – King Henry IV and his consort, Queen Joan of Navarre; Nicholas Wootton, who became the first Dean of Canterbury in 1542; William Courtenay, Archbishop of Canterbury between 1381 and 1396; and the Black Prince (at whose requiem mass William Courtenay officiated). It is curious that such an historically significant site should have been chosen and permitted for the temporary resting place of a visiting French Cardinal, even after the shrine of Becket had been swept away. It is even more curious not only that the body was never repatriated (though it is true that Coligny fell violently from favour in his native France), but that it continued to remain in the Trinity Chapel as its permanent resting place long after all possibility of repatriation had dissolved, even to the extent of being given a protective shell of plaster and hessian.

A second suggested location for the burial of Becket's bones was made in 1892 by the director of the Society of Antiquaries, Mr Milman.[11] He proposed the 'corona' at the eastern end of the Trinity Chapel as the true site. Milman based his case partly on Thomas Derby's statement, drafted in 1539, in which he asserted that the saint's bones 'shuld be taken away and bestowed in suche place as the same shuld cause no superstition afterwards ... and buried in a noble toure', and partly on the possibility that Cardinal Reginald Pole might have chosen the corona as his own final resting place because he knew that Becket's remains were also there.

The corona, with its ambiguous meaning, undoubtedly occupies a special place in the hagiography of Becket. Nevertheless, Milman's case does not appear to be a very strong one, and it has not found favour with other antiquarians. It requires a nimble exercise of the imagination to suppose that the corona is the most obvious place in the Cathedral to merit the description of 'a noble toure', and Milman's argument about

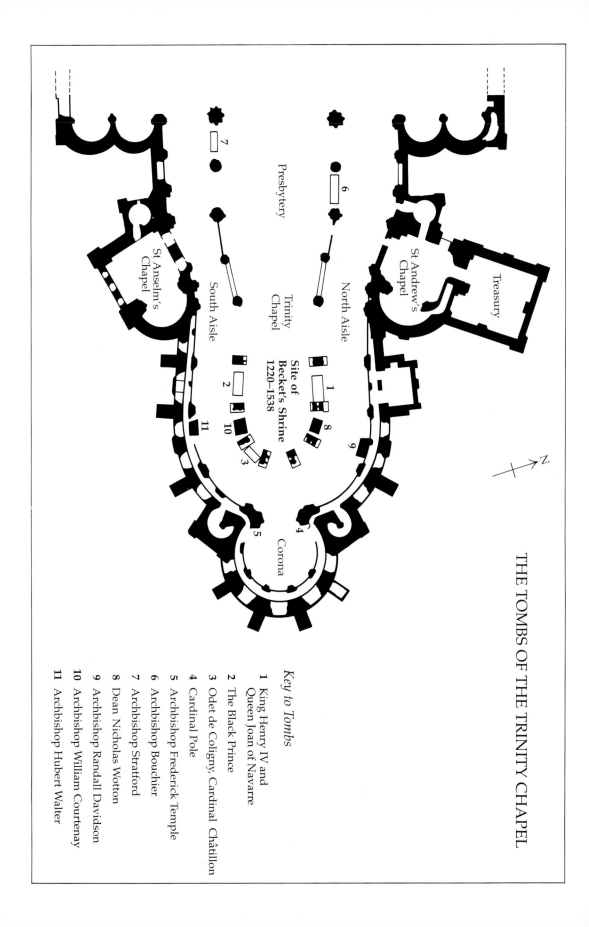

THE TOMBS OF THE TRINITY CHAPEL

Treasury

St Andrew's
Chapel

St Anselm's
Chapel

Presbytery

Trinity
Chapel

North Aisle

South Aisle

Site of
Becket's Shrine
1220–1538

Corona

N

Key to Tombs

1 King Henry IV and
   Queen Joan of Navarre
2 The Black Prince
3 Odet de Coligny, Cardinal Châtillon
4 Cardinal Pole
5 Archbishop Frederick Temple
6 Archbishop Bouchier
7 Archbishop Stratford
8 Dean Nicholas Wotton
9 Archbishop Randall Davidson
10 Archbishop William Courtenay
11 Archbishop Hubert Walter

Cardinal Pole is circumstantial, to say the least. The argument was not that Pole actually requested to be buried in the vicinity of Becket, merely that his choice of the corona (where a relic that the monks claimed to be Becket's head had been kept) in preference to the crypt (where the whole of his body had undoubtedly been kept for fifty years between 1170 and 1220) implied that Pole had special reasons for choosing the former.

A third possible location for the burial of Becket's bones is the monks' cemetery that lay to the east and south-east of the Cathedral. There is a strong element of common sense in this: the best place in which to hide something is among many others of the same sort. If the monks did indeed remove the bones from the shrine with intent to conceal them from the Commissioners, then the cemetery would not only be a highly convenient and appropriate hiding place, it would almost certainly guarantee the bones' concealment for as long as might be required. Of course, the site would have to be left unmarked, and a small number of the monks would have to remember it if they intended later to disinter the bones and move them to a more appropriate place. As a short-term repository for the saint's relics, however, the cemetery might be thought to hold a great deal of attraction.

It is not only common sense that points towards the cemetery; there is also the suggestive language in the narrative of William Thomas.[12] 'Butt this is true,' he is supposed to have claimed, 'that his bones are spred amongest the bones of so many dead men, that without some greate miracle they will not be found agayne.' Milman interpreted this to mean that Becket's bones were buried (in the corona) alongside those of other saints who were similarly unshrined or untombed in 1538. Yet a better interpretation might well be a cemetery, where 'the bones of so many dead men' are to be found, and where a newly interred and unmarked set of bones might well not be found again 'without some greate miracle'.

A fourth possible location is the north transept of the crypt. There, in front of the adjacent apsidal Chapels of St Mary Magdalene and St Nicholas, are what appear to be two graves, side by side. One is covered by an irregularly shaped slab embossed with what looks to be the cross of Canterbury atop a staff; the other, immediately to the south of it, is indicated by the disturbance to the pavement, suggesting that an excavation has been made to permit a burial beneath. No official knowledge seems to exist about the nature of these two supposed graves: a recent authoritative guide to the Cathedral, for example, postulated that the unidentified slab 'may well have come from some destroyed thirteenth century tomb, since it does not appear to cover a grave of any kind'.[13]

The belief that Becket's bones may lie in one or other of these putative

Plan of the tombs in the Trinity Chapel.

graves is persistent, though the evidence is no more than circumstantial. There is, first, the curious fact that the embossed slab covering one of the supposed graves is almost identical to that covering the tomb of Archbishop Stephen Langton in another part of the Cathedral.[14] Then there is the further curiosity of the red sanctuary lamp that burns above the altar in the Chapel of St Mary Magdalene, only a few feet away from the two supposed graves. Red being the symbolic colour of martyrdom, such a lamp might, in the absence of the reserved sacrament, normally be expected to denote a place of particular significance for a martyr of the Christian faith. Yet there seems to be no commonly agreed explanation for the presence of the red lamp so close to the two apparent burial sites.

In addition to circumstantial evidence of this kind, there are also assorted stories that link the north crypt transept with Becket's final place of burial. Such stories, though persistent, are unsubstantiated, and can be taken as evidence of nothing more than the myths that are current at any particular time. Visitors to the Cathedral may hear that Becket's relics are lying in one of the two graves, and various suggestions have been advanced about the possible occupant of the other one. Some say that it is William Petham, a prior of Christ Church who entertained King Edward IV and his wife, Elizabeth, during a visit to Canterbury in September 1471 and who died almost exactly a year later; but William Somner, in his *Antiquities of Canterbury* published in 1703, stated explicitly that Petham's burial place is unknown.[15] Others, including David Sox in his book *Relics and Shrines*, claim that it is Edward Grim, the clerk who attended Becket at his martyrdom and parried the first blow from one of the knights. Sox asserted that this story 'has been quietly repeated by a number of clerics', one of whom was said to have told him that 'it was the interpretation of events given by Archdeacon Julian Bickersteth'.[16] Bickersteth is of obvious interest in this context since he was also named by the pseudonymous 'Thomas Chough' in 1990 as one who knew the true resting place of Becket's relics and who knew also of the coterie of those who pray there twice a year.[17]

Julian Bickersteth was five years older than his colleague on the Chapter, Canon John Shirley. He was born into a distinguished family in 1885, the third of four remarkable sons of the Reverend Dr Samuel Bickersteth. The eldest was Bishop in Egypt and Sudan between 1920 and 1974; the next eldest was Regius Professor of English Literature in the University of Aberdeen between 1938 and 1954; and the youngest captained the Oxford University Association Football team in 1910 and was later warden of Hart House, in the University of Toronto, between 1921 and 1947.

Julian Bickersteth was educated at Rugby School and Christ Church,

The Chapels of St Mary Magdalen (showing the red sanctuary lamp) (left) and St Nicholas in the crypt.

Oxford. Having trained at Wells Theological College, he served as senior chaplain to the 56th Territorial Division on the Western Front, where he was awarded the MC and was twice mentioned in dispatches. He spent the post-war years as headmaster of St Peter's Collegiate School in Adelaide, returning to England in 1933 to become headmaster of Felsted School in Essex for ten years. He then moved to Canterbury on being appointed Canon Residentiary of the Cathedral and Archdeacon of Maidstone, posts that he held until four years before his death in 1962. Bickersteth was also treasurer of Canterbury Cathedral between 1945 and 1958.

Throughout the 1950s, Bickersteth and Shirley came to play a crucial part in the affairs of Canterbury Cathedral and its Chapter as the Dean, Dr Hewlett Johnson, increasingly withdrew himself from the local scene. Though also headmaster of the King's School, Shirley was intimately involved in all the day-to-day issues in the precincts,[18] even to the extent of becoming treasurer of the Cathedral in 1958 in succession to Julian Bickersteth and librarian in 1961. As noted in Chapter 6, it was Shirley who corresponded with Mr Emden, the principal of St Edmund Hall, about the re-exhumation of the bones in the eastern crypt in 1949; it was he who was instructed by the Chapter to enquire about the possibility of dating the bones; and it was under his name that the summary of Professor Cave's report appeared in *The Times* in August 1951.[19]

The relationship between Shirley and Bickersteth is not entirely clear. According to Sox, they had 'little time for each other',[20] but Edwards suggests otherwise in his sympathetic biography of Shirley.[21] Though Bickersteth was not, according to Edwards, Shirley's closest colleague on the Chapter, he had much to do with Shirley not only through the Chapter, but also in his position as honorary chaplain to the King's School. He 'cheered its headmaster on with his own zest'[22] and enjoyed a brotherly, pastoral relationship with him.

Whether acting in collaboration or not, Shirley and Bickersteth became engaged during the 1950s in remarkably similar courses of action which suggest, circumstantially but tantalisingly, that they may have had their own views about the two putative graves in the Chapels of St Mary Magdalene and St Nicholas. The facts, as set out in the *Minutes of the Canterbury Chapter*, are straightforward. In May 1951, as noted in Chapter 6, the Dean and Chapter received the report from Professor Cave showing conclusively that the bones he examined could not have been those of Becket. In June the Chapter recorded its final minute on the matter.[23] At the very next meeting of the Chapter, Shirley raised the question of replacing the altars in the Chapels of St Mary Magdalene and St Nicholas.[24] For the next five years work proceeded on the refurbishment

The tomb of Odet de Coligny (Cardinal Châtillon) in the Trinity Chapel.

of the two chapels, the *Minutes of the Canterbury Chapter* containing various references to their design, construction and positioning.

Part of the cost of the refurbishments was borne personally by Shirley and Bickersteth. Shirley donated the altar and predella in the Chapel of St Mary Magdalene (1955), together with the red sanctuary lamp (1956) and the altar crucifix (1959). Bickersteth, together with his brothers, furnished the adjacent Chapel of St Nicholas (1956) and donated the altar (1957) in thanksgiving for their parents' long association with Canterbury. (The Reverend Dr Samuel Bickersteth, the father, had been a canon of Canterbury between 1916 and 1936.) The altar was used for the first time in May 1958, and a week later a plaque was unveiled nearby in memory of Canon Samuel Bickersteth and his wife, Ella.

In July 1958 Shirley celebrated the first holy communion in the newly refurbished Chapel of St Mary Magdalene. He died in July 1967, and his funeral took place in the Cathedral four days later. His body was cremated and the ashes were interred in the Chapel of St Mary Magdalene. The place of the interment, immediately to the south of the altar and a few feet away from the two conjectured graves, is marked by a small plaque set in the floor of the apse.

This sequence of events does not provide direct evidence that either Bickersteth or Shirley may have had special knowledge about the two graves in the Chapels of St Mary Magdalene and St Nicholas, or about a link between them and the grave in the eastern crypt. It may have been a simple coincidence that, at Shirley's suggestion, the Chapter turned its attention to the refurbishment of the two chapels as soon as the grave in the eastern crypt was finally closed; and the parallel decisions of Bickersteth and Shirley to bear much of the cost of the refurbishment themselves may simply have been the wholly understandable responses of two men who doubtless loved and honoured the Cathedral. It was certainly not the first occasion on which members of the staff of the Cathedral had contributed privately to the maintenance of the fabric. In any case, Bickersteth had been a Fellow of the Corporation of St Mary and St Nicholas since 1943, suggesting that his interest in the two chapels pre-dated the investigations in 1949–51.

The facts do, however, bear an alternative, speculative interpretation. It requires the assumption that somehow the two men acquired information between about 1948 and 1951 that led them to believe that the true remains of Becket were not, after all, in the grave in the eastern crypt but in one of the two putative burial sites in the Chapels of Saints Mary Magdalene and Nicholas. Information might, for example, have come to them in Mr Emden's letter to Shirley in February 1949 which triggered the Chapter's decision to reopen the grave in the eastern crypt.[25] This could explain the otherwise puzzling decision of the Chapter to seek a modern scientific opinion on the identity of the bones within a matter of weeks of looking at a commissioned design for a tomb in which to house them. It might also provide a credible reason for Bickersteth and Shirley's wishes to contribute personally to the refurbishment of the two altars; and it could explain the red sanctuary lamp, endowed by Shirley, that burns above the altar of St Mary Magdalene.

This account is itself replete with difficulties. What was the nature of the information, if such it was, that led them to suppose that the remains of Becket were reposing in one of the two graves? How could these two experienced and senior churchmen have been sufficiently satisfied about its likely veracity to persuade them to take the dramatic step of reopening the grave in the eastern crypt? And why, if they became convinced of its truth, did they decide to honour the resting place of the saint as an act of private and personal commemoration rather than, as might seem much more natural, by persuading the Chapter to investigate the graves in the north crypt transept with a view to erecting the tomb of St Thomas there?

This second hypothesis raises even more difficulties than the first, though it ought not on that ground alone to be avoided. By denying any connection between Becket and the grave in the eastern crypt, this hypothesis, like the first, is obliged to suggest an identity for the skeleton that takes account of the seemingly hasty, furtive and careless circumstances surrounding its retrieval from an earth grave and its interment in the crypt. No obvious solution takes adequate account of all the findings reported by Professor Cave. Moreover, this second hypothesis is also obliged to find a plausible resting place for the true remains of Becket, where they were supposedly placed by the monks of the priory in 1538. There is no shortage of suggested sites, merely of safe or satisfactory evidence for any of them.

Hypothesis 3: that Becket's bones were buried by the Commissioners in collaboration with the monks, and that there is no connection between Becket and the '1888 grave site'

The third hypothesis is a subsidiary of the second: it assumes that no connection exists between the fate of Becket's bones in 1538 and the skeleton in the crypt, but it postulates that the saint's remains were buried not by the monks in secret but by the King's Commissioners in collusion with the priory. In essence, it involves more or less the same possibilities and the same difficulties as those just discussed. It would, however, rule out the tomb of Cardinal Châtillon as a possible site, since he did not die until thirty-three years after the Commissioners had done their business. It might also increase the likelihood that the bones were removed entirely from Canterbury, probably to the Tower of London, whither those of other unshrined saints were apparently taken.

Hypothesis 4: that Becket's bones were buried secretly by the monks in 1538, and that there is a connection between Becket and the '1888 grave site'

The fourth hypothesis, like the second, assumes that Becket's bones were not burned in 1538 but were buried secretly by the monks. Unlike the second hypothesis, however, it asserts that some kind of connection exists between Becket and the grave in the eastern crypt – a connection that might provide a clue to its identification. Three main connections can be imagined.

First, it is possible that the coffin in the crypt did originally contain the remains of the saint, where they were placed in haste by the monks but later removed and replaced by the bones that were discovered in 1888. There is much to be said for this theory. If the monks did remove the saint's remains from the shrine before the King's Commissioners arrived, and if the act was done in secrecy and haste, then much of what is otherwise inexplicable about the grave in the eastern crypt falls into place. The monks may have intended from the outset that it should be no more than a temporary resting place, offering short-term concealment until a more permanent solution could be arranged. If so, the ill-suited coffin, which may have been crudely adapted from the nearest available vessel, and its shallow depth of burial, can be conveniently explained.

This sequence of events is not implausible; indeed, most of those who believed in the authenticity of the skeleton between 1888 and 1951 appear to have been impressed not only by the skeleton itself but also by the position and features of the grave. Among those who found nothing intrinsically odd about the notion that Becket's bones might once have filled the coffin were the Dean and members of the Chapter, who in 1948 were preparing to erect a tomb on the site. The fact that they were mistaken in their views about the identification of the skeleton does not detract at all from their assessment of the significance of the grave itself, for there was nothing in Professor Cave's report that would exclude its use for such a purpose.

Thus far, the idea has credibility: the remains of Becket were taken from the shrine by the monks some time before September 1538, deposited initially in the grave in the eastern crypt, and later removed for permanent burial elsewhere – either in one of the places suggested earlier in this chapter or in another place of which no rumour has been heard. But when was the switch done, and whose bones were used to replace those of the Archbishop in the makeshift coffin, and why?

There are no satisfactory answers to these questions, only speculation. If the monks did remove the bones from the shrine and secrete them in the shallow grave in the eastern crypt in some haste, replacing them in the shrine with others that were eventually burned, then those who knew of the secret may later have had reasons for believing that the clandestine grave would be discovered and the true relics taken away. Such a belief may have been well founded. At a meeting of the Privy Council at Hull in October 1541, the King issued a letter to all the bishops, through Archbishop Cranmer, expressing his displeasure that 'the shrines, coverings of shrines and monuments of such things yet remain in sundry places'.[26] He instructed the bishops to search their cathedrals and 'if any such thing remains, to take it away'. The injunction did not specifically include the relics of saints, but those who knew the secret of the grave may have believed its contents to be in danger. If so, they would have moved swiftly to remove the real bones from their grave in the eastern crypt and restock it with other human remains that could, if necessary, be passed off as those of someone else. Any old bones might do for a subterfuge of this kind: they could have been dug up hastily and carelessly (earth, debris and all) from another burial place. It might have been the monks' cemetery, for which the legendary precedent would be the action of the monks at Durham; or it might, in view of the fact that the original burial had been directly in the earth, have been a common public grave. The assortment of animal bones mixed up with those of the skeleton in the coffin suggests that the common grave, if that is what it was, might have adjoined a market where animal carcasses were butchered. Whatever the source, the skeleton (on this interpretation of events) was of no one of any significance, whose identity will never now be known.

This account provides a reasonably satisfactory explanation for a number of elements that otherwise remain mysterious: not only the curious features of the grave and its coffin, but also the marks borne by the skeleton of a hasty and careless exhumation from its original burial place. Yet it also poses difficulties. Most obviously, why, if the monks were really intent on concealing Becket's remains from the Commissioners, did they not bury them immediately in a secret final resting place? And even if, for some reason, temporary concealment was necessary, why did they choose a place that would almost invite the attention of anyone intent on sniffing out suspected deception?

Answers to these questions may be found in a second explanation linking Becket with the grave in the crypt. Like the first, it assumes that the monks removed the bones from the shrine some time before the arrival of the King's Commissioners, but it differs in asserting that the place chosen in the crypt for their concealment was intended from the outset to be a permanent and final one. Any such intention would, of course, account very well for the choice of the site, with its intimate associations with the murdered Archbishop. The monks, that is to say, may have buried the bones in a normal coffin at an ordinary depth, where they remain to this day. The existence of the '1888 coffin' above the 'true' resting place of Becket can, as in the first connection, be explained quite simply as a decoy. Should those who knew the secret have had reason to believe that the deception was about to be discovered (for example through some such search as that ordered by the King in his letter to Cranmer in 1541), then the simplest method of concealment would be by the insertion into the grave site of a second, innocent coffin. The skeleton it contained could, if discovered in the course of a search, be passed off either as that of someone of no significance, or perhaps even as that of Becket himself. Such an admittedly risky deception would be aided by selecting a skull that had obviously suffered severe damage, and also by arranging the bones in a manner similar to that in which they might have been placed in the shrine. If the bluff was called and the decoy bones were burned, it would be of no consequence to the monks.

If the decoy bones had to be secreted in haste, an obvious course of action would be a visit either to the monks' cemetery outside the Cathedral or to a communal grave. Such an action, as noted earlier, would satisfactorily account for the spade-marks found on the skeleton, for the missing bones, and for the presence in the coffin of extraneous earth, debris and animal remains.

There is a further twist to this explanation – the coffin of the Abbot of Evesham, William de Audeville. If Beazeley was correct in his assertion that the Abbot had been buried in this place in 1159,[27] the monks would probably have found the coffin in the course of digging out the grave. It is possible, in view of the haste that may have been required, that, rather than remove the Abbot's coffin before inserting Becket's, they merely laid one upon the other. The space above Becket's coffin would then be restricted, forcing the third (decoy) coffin to lie only a few inches beneath the surface. The legendary claim in the Chronicles of the Abbots of Evesham that 'the blessed Thomas the Martyr was buried at his [de Audeville's] feet' would, among those in the know, acquire an astonishing new meaning.

There is no record that the Portland stone coffin was ever removed from the ground in either the 1888 or 1949 excavations. With hindsight, this is an obvious cause for regret. Had the ground beneath the coffin been explored, there is an outside (but obviously staggering) possibility that two further coffins might have been uncovered: first that of Becket, and then that of William de Audeville.

A third explanation linking Becket with the grave in the crypt is rather different to the first two. It hinges on the interesting possibility that those who placed the '1888 bones' in the coffin *genuinely but mistakenly* believed them to be those of the saint. This might account for the choice of the site, adjacent to that of Becket's original tomb; but in what circumstances could such an act have taken place? A possible answer has already been suggested. One of the locations that might have been selected by the monks for temporary concealment of the bones is the cemetery that lay to the east and south-east of the Cathedral. It would offer an almost foolproof place of hiding for human remains, and it is hinted at in William Thomas's assertion that 'his bones are spread amongst the bones of so many dead men'. Of course, the site of interment would have to be left unmarked, which might frustrate any attempt to recover the bones for a more suitable permanent burial elsewhere. Just such an attempt would offer a plausible account for the interment of the wrong bones in the crypt. If Becket's remains had indeed been buried initially in the monks' cemetery, and if a later attempt had been made to exhume them for reburial close to the spot where Becket's tomb had stood in the crypt, then it is perhaps not too fanciful to see that the wrong skeleton may have been exhumed (in the genuinely mistaken belief about its identity) and placed in the coffin in the eastern crypt. The fact that the exhumation seems to have been done with such haste, maybe even under cover of darkness, would add to the likelihood of genuine error; and the visible damage to the skull might be taken as further evidence that the right set of bones had been dug up. The haste and secrecy of the operation would also explain the reason for the initial, shallow burial in the crypt in an ill-suited coffin; and any intention to remove the remains to a more suitable final resting place might have been thwarted by the walling off of the eastern crypt in 1546.

As with every other hypothesis, there are problems with this also. Is it really credible that anyone who thought they were exhuming the remains of the great martyr would have done so with (as Professor Cave put it) 'gross and destructive carelessness'? Would they have had such little reverence for the relics as to allow them to be mixed up in the coffin with an assortment of animal bones? If the initial burial place in the crypt was intended to be a temporary one, why was such a highly significant site chosen? And why was no attempt made later to relocate the remains even though the first beneficiary of the walled-off eastern crypt was Richard Thornden, a former monk of the priory who remained loyal to the Roman Catholic cause and who must presumably have known about the existence of the grave? These difficulties may be sufficiently weighty to discount the whole idea of a genuine mistake.

Hypothesis 5: that Becket's bones were buried by the Commissioners in collaboration with the monks, and that there is a connection between Becket and the '1888 grave site'

The final hypothesis asserts that, as in the third hypothesis, the remains of Becket were buried quietly and discreetly by the Commissioners in 1538; but it differs in assuming a connection between this action and the skeleton exhumed from the crypt in 1888. What could that connection have been? Two possibilities suggest themselves.

The Commissioners, acting in collaboration with the monks, may have selected the grave in the eastern crypt as their chosen place in which to bestow the bones of the saint, and may actually have done so. Such a choice of burial place would be consistent with the practice elsewhere of interring the bones of unshrined saints near, or beneath, the sites of their erstwhile shrines. From this point of view, the choice of this particular place in the eastern crypt, with its intimate associations with Becket, might be an obvious one.

If this occurred, the true remains of the saint might still be there, concealed beneath the '1888 coffin'. They could not have been discovered in either 1888 or 1949 because the coffin was not lifted and the ground beneath it explored. But if so, how can the '1888 coffin' be accounted for? In what circumstances might a crudely exhumed set of bones be placed in an unsuitable coffer and buried directly above the site of the grave of a saint? Credible explanations are hard to imagine unless some further deception is assumed. Perhaps someone who knew that the true remains of Becket were in that grave (having been placed there by the Commissioners) later decided to remove them for some unknown purpose and wished to cover the tracks by resorting to a decoy coffin. After all, the eastern crypt was effectively a place of private access between 1546 and 1838, perhaps rendering it vulnerable to such an act of predation. But if so, who did the dreadful deed, and when, and why? Where were the bones removed to, and where are they now?

The second possibility is that the bones of Becket, having been removed from the shrine by the Commissioners, were placed in the '1888 coffin' but were later removed for some purpose and replaced by the substitute bones that were found in 1888. This possibility might account quite well for the choice of the site, and also for the crude nature of the coffin – the Commissioners having been more concerned that the bones were simply out of the way than that they were interred in a fitting receptacle. The shallow depth of the burial of the coffin may simply reflect the fact that the water level beneath the floor of the crypt is high, precluding any interment at a more normal depth. (Miss Holland, who witnessed the first exhumation of the bones in 1888, recalled that the workmen who were excavating the eastern crypt were 'splashing in water' in their trenches).[28] The fact that the coffin of the Abbot of Evesham might already have been occupying the site would place a further restriction on the depth to which the Commissioners could go.

This hypothesis also gives rise to a number of almost intractable questions. Why, if the Commissioners had initially been intent on burying the relics in that site, did they not abandon it as soon as they discovered the Abbot of Evesham's coffin? Who could have gone to the extraordinarily elaborate lengths of removing the bones of the saint from their sanctioned resting place and replacing them with others that had been hastily dug up from a common burial ground? What might have been the motive? When could it have been done? What happened to the real bones? At the end of all the questions, there remains a mystery.

Henry does penance at the tomb in the crypt 11 June 1174:
from a window in the north aisle of the Trinity Chapel.

9 A Mystery

As much through the circumstances of his death as through the paradoxes of his life, St Thomas Becket has exercised a fascination in the minds of those who encounter his story. His martyrdom in 1170 shook the medieval Church to its roots and has since become popularised as one of the great and dramatic events of European history, known even to countless people who have never visited Canterbury and who may not be sure exactly why he died. Together with Augustine and Chaucer, Becket has, through the manner of his dying, shaped the history of Canterbury in a way that few others have done, ensuring that Canterbury Cathedral is universally known as the church in which murder was done and to which the medieval pilgrims came in their droves.

The pilgrimages ended with the Reformation, but the memorials of Becket have lived on. So, too, has an interest in his relics, the history of which has sometimes been more than a matter merely of antiquarian curiosity or public fascination. The persistent debate about the fate of Becket's bones throughout the last hundred years has been set in an ecclesiastical context that is bound to have shaped the views and predispositions of those engaged in it. The extraordinary intensity of interest in the identity of the bones discovered in 1888, and the very highest levels at which it was pursued for over sixty years, is evidence of the passions and perhaps even the fears that the relics of the martyr could still evoke. Sometimes driven as much by their personal dispositions as by the evidence itself, those who participated in the debate about the identity of the skeleton taken from the grave in the eastern crypt interpreted and used the data in ways that supported their own predilections, whether for or against the 'Becket hypothesis'. For the most part, they saw in the bones exactly what they wished to see.

But in the last decade of the twentieth century the ecclesiastical and religious significance of the relics has shifted. Were the true bones of Becket to appear now (difficult though it is to imagine how such an incontestable appearance might occur), the consequences might be more severe for tourist managers than for theologians or church politicians; and any interest that the public may have in them is now more likely to

156

be driven by secular curiosity than by religious devotion. In a predominantly unchurched society, the relics of saints may hold little attraction as objects of veneration or as potential agents of miraculous events. Those who visit, say, the tomb of St Cuthbert at Durham or the shrine of St Edward at Westminster are, for the most part, unlikely to do so for the same reasons that sent generations of medieval pilgrims flocking to Canterbury; nor are they likely to be struck by the paradox of the continuing existence of the remains of Catholic saints in Protestant churches. Of the great English medieval shrines, only Walsingham has been restored as a focus of regular pilgrimages, and these are increasingly being undertaken in an ecumenical spirit.

If there is any continuing public interest in the bones of Becket, the reason is likely to be the natural human one of fascination with significant things of the past. Eight centuries after his death, Becket is still a charismatic figure in the historical imagination of the western world, and the authentication of any artefacts associated with him is bound to be a source of widespread curiosity. It is the same kind of fascination that was generated in Rome in April 1992 by the opening of a reliquary containing what purported to be a linen tunic that had been worn by Becket (though not at the time of his death) and that was sprinkled with his blood. The tunic, which had been kept in the Basilica of Santa Maria Maggiore, was subjected to testing by two scientists from the University of Munich, Professors Ursula Nilgen and Leonie von Wilckens, who concluded that 'its authenticity can be considered a great certainty'. Understandably, the authentication was the cause of much interest: here, in the late twentieth century, was an artefact from the distant past that had probably been in intimate contact with one of the great figures of history.

If the authentication of one of Becket's garments can stir the popular imagination, even more so would the discovery and authentication of his true relics. It is no surprise that the quest for Becket's bones has continued for many years, or that many myths and legends have grown up about their resting place. Visitors to Canterbury Cathedral who enquire about the fate of the saint's remains are liable to be plied with a number of incompatible stories, some of which must be wrong. They include stories about the burning as well as the burial of the saint's bones. Some of these stories have been reproduced above, since myths and rumours are of great importance as social facts; but a clear attempt has always been made to distinguish unfounded assertions from those that can be supported by a modicum of evidence, however circumstantial.

A great many elements in the story can reasonably be treated as facts. Thomas Becket, Archbishop of Canterbury, died in Canterbury Cathedral in December 1170 as the result of severe head wounds. At least

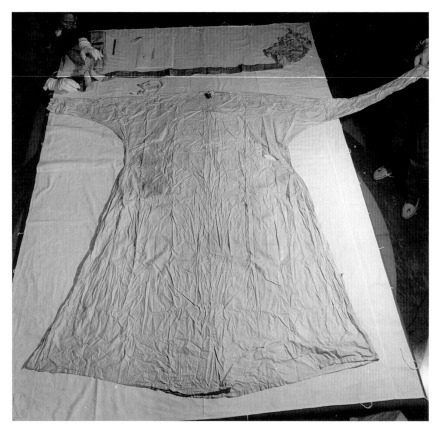

The linen tunic, kept in the Basilica of Santa Maria Maggiore in Rome and authenticated by scientists as having been worn by Becket .

one of the sword blows that killed him opened an aperture in the cranial vault. His body rested overnight in front of the high altar of the Cathedral before being buried the following day in a marble or stone coffin in what was then the Chapel of the Holy Trinity at the extreme eastern end of the crypt. The body was later removed from the coffin on at least one occasion and secreted elsewhere in the crypt to prevent its theft, but it was returned to the original coffin when the danger had passed. Eventually a sort of tomb was erected over the burial site, partly for protection and security. The tomb, which survived the great fire of 1174, was finally located in the new eastern crypt between the eastern-most two of the three Purbeck marble pillars in the central aisle.

In July 1220, the body (or, more probably, the bones) was again taken from the coffin in the eastern crypt. A number of small bones were kept aside, and the remainder, almost certainly including the skull, were deposited inside the gilded and bejewelled shrine standing in the recently completed Trinity Chapel at the eastern end of the Cathedral. The relics remained in the shrine, undisturbed, until 1538. In September of that year, Commissioners acting under instruction from the King removed the bones of the saint from the shrine, which was destroyed. No authentic record has come to hand either of the mandate given to the Commissioners or of their method of disposal of the bones. A document that purports to contain a royal mandate to burn the bones of Becket, and that reports its execution, is generally regarded by historians as false.

Within about a month of the destruction of the shrine, in October 1538, the Pope announced in Rome that the King had ordered Becket's body to be burned and the ashes scattered to the winds. The papal announcement did not assert that the burning had actually taken place, merely that it had been ordered by the King. A few weeks later, in December 1538, a bull of excommunication against the King repeated the claim that he had ordered the burning. Within a very short time the story was being told in many places in Europe that the bones of Becket, together with those of other unshrined saints, had been consigned to the flames.

In England, two different stories arose about the fate accorded to the saint's remains. One, which was told by the English chroniclers Wriothesley, Stow and Holinshed, claimed that the remains had been burned in Canterbury Cathedral by (or in the presence of) the Lord Privy Seal, Thomas Cromwell. The same story, without the reference to Cromwell, was told by Nicholas Harpsfield, the Roman Catholic Archdeacon of Canterbury in the reign of Queen Mary Tudor. The alternative story held that the saint's remains had not in fact been burned but had been buried in a place that would not give rise to their continuing veneration. This story, which may have been associated with an attempt on the part of the King to justify his actions, had more than one strand. One strand asserted that the bones had been buried in a noble tower; the other that they had been buried in a place containing many other bones.

In 1888 an almost complete skeleton was uncovered in the eastern crypt of Canterbury Cathedral, next to the site where Becket's body had been buried for fifty years between 1170 and 1220. The skeleton was lying a few inches beneath the surface in a vessel that appeared not to have been intended for use as a coffin. The report of a local surgeon who examined the skeleton identified it as that of a large man, about 50 years of age, with one major and several lesser fractures to the skull. A national debate sprang up about the identity of the skeleton, which continued for many years. Opinion was divided on whether it might be the skeleton of Becket. Those who held that it was, were impressed by the size, age and antiquity of the man whose skeleton it was, by the large wound in the skull which might have been caused by a sharp cutting instrument such as a sword, and by the place in which the coffin had been found, immediately adjacent to Becket's first grave. Those who rejected the skeleton as that of the saint relied on two major arguments: that the true remains of Becket had been burned in 1538, and that the wounds in the skull were incompatible with the contemporary accounts of the manner of his death.

By 1920, following a comprehensive and scholarly review of all the relevant evidence commissioned by the then Archbishop of Canterbury, opinion seemed on balance to favour the view that the skeleton was that of Becket. Dissenting views were still expressed, however. By the late 1940s the Dean and Chapter had accepted its authenticity and had commissioned a design for a tomb to contain (or at least protect) the contents of the grave in the eastern crypt. But the tomb of Becket was never built, and instead the Dean and Chapter authorised the reopening of the grave for the purpose of a new scientific assessment of the bones. The skeleton was re-exhumed in 1949 and subjected for two years to detailed examination by scientists working at St Bartholomew's Hospital in London. The report of the examination, submitted to the Dean and Chapter in May 1951, concluded that the bones could not have been those of Becket. A major piece of supporting evidence (though not the only one) was the fact that none of the fractures in the skull had been caused prior to death. The report also contained evidence that the skeleton had at one time been buried directly in the earth as a whole body, and had later been dug up with great haste or carelessness before being reinterred in the site where it was discovered in 1888.

The 1951 report was never made available to the public, though a partial summary of it was published in *The Times* and in a local journal. The summary emphasised the negative conclusion that the skeleton was not that of Becket, but did not highlight the positive findings about its earlier earth burial and the carelessness of its exhumation. Following the 1951 report, stories continued to circulate about the fate of Becket's bones, sometimes (but not usually) in published form. In 1990 a pseudonymous allegation was made in a local newspaper that the true burial place of Becket's remains was known to a small number of people. Two names were mentioned in this context of men who, though by then dead, had been associated with the debate about the identification of the 1888 skeleton.

These appear to be established facts. Their sources have all been listed in the foregoing chapters, and they can be checked and confirmed by any interested person. They seem to point towards two clear, if disappointingly negative, conclusions. First, the evidence about the disposal of

Becket's bones in 1538 is insufficiently conclusive to affirm that they were either buried or burned. The only safe position permitted by the evidence is one of agnosticism: the truth cannot be determined on the strict basis of the documentation that has come down to us. Secondly, the correct identity of the person whose skeleton was discovered in the eastern crypt in 1888 cannot be discerned. That it was not Thomas Becket is indisputable; but the evidence is insufficient to permit any other definite identification. When all is said and done, the mystery remains.

From the fastidious perspective of the purist, dependent on the evidence alone, this is all that can safely be said about the matter (though it is perhaps worth noting that such a perspective would find fault with those who tell the story of the burning of the bones and the scattering of their ashes in the wind, or in the River Stour, or through the barrel of a cannon, as though it were an historically established fact). But those who have pursued the evidence thus far have usually pushed beyond the safe position of agnosticism towards one of commitment – one way or the other. Very few who have written about the fate of Becket's bones, or about the identity of the skeleton in the eastern crypt, have ceased their writing at the point of doubt: with few exceptions (and for reasons best known to themselves) they have bravely, or rashly, declared their own subjective conclusions from the material they have reviewed.

For those who accept the evidence that the bones were burned in 1538, there is little of value left to debate. The identity of the skeleton in the eastern crypt remains a puzzle, but, since it cannot be linked in any way with the treatment accorded to Becket's relics, it is not one that merits much attention. In any case, the true identity is now unlikely ever to be known. For those who are disinclined uncritically to accept the evidence for the burning, however, a number of questions continue to intrigue.

The central question is that of the fate of Becket's bones when his shrine was destroyed in 1538. It would not be unreasonable to conclude that they are as likely to have been buried as burned. No authentic royal mandate for the burning has come to light, and the assorted accounts in the English chronicles of the removal of the remains from the shrine, and their subsequent consumption by fire, post-date the event by several years. Extant Commissions for other places make no mention of burning as the required method of disposing of saintly remains, (though many other kinds of objects were certainly burned), and the contemporary documents and letters do not suggest that they usually suffered such a fate. In some cases the offending bones were required to be removed to the Tower of London, and in others they seem to have been disposed of at the discretion of the local Commissioners. A discreet and unmarked burial elsewhere in the Cathedral appears to have been a common solution to the problem.

The rumour of burning at Canterbury originated in Rome, first at the consistory held in October 1538 and then in the following month in the papal bull of excommunication against the King. The charge was not that the bones of Becket had actually been burned, merely that the King had ordered it. Once the story had been given papal authority, it is hardly surprising that it began to spread throughout Europe and that the command became the act: Becket's bones had been burned. In time the story was repeated by the English chroniclers, who added extra details about the state of the skull, about the site of the burning, and about the presence of Cromwell in the Cathedral that did not appear in the continental versions.

Constant repetition of a story, however, is no guarantee of its authenticity. The central question is whether the Pope was correctly informed in the first place not only of the King's command but also of its execution. Of this there is no direct evidence. If he was misinformed, for example by being led to believe that the faked skull that was probably burned at Canterbury was that of Becket, then the subsequent repetition and spreading of the story, though wholly understandable, would count for nothing.

The position adopted by the Dean and Chapter in 1948–9 may not carry quite as much weight as might at first be thought. While they rejected the hypothesis of burning by their acceptance of the skeleton in the eastern crypt as that of Becket, even to the extent of making advanced arrangements for the erection of a tomb to house the bones, it may be unrealistic to conclude that they reached their decision on the basis of a careful and scholarly weighing of the evidence. On the other hand, the testimony of Nicholas Harpsfield, Archdeacon of Canterbury during the Marian period, does appear at face value to constitute substantial evidence in favour of the burning: he must surely have known the true fate of the bones, and he wrote clearly that they had been burned. Whether he was an altogether reliable witness may, however, be disputed. Townsend said of him that 'whoever will take the trouble to read Harpsfield will find that he is very diffuse and indefinite'.[1] For example, Harpsfield claimed that the bones of St Augustine had also been burned in Canterbury,[2] although no corroborating evidence exists in the contemporary documentation.[3] Harpsfield's testimony about the fate of Becket's bones was contradicted, seemingly with intent, by an anonymous author known only as Ro:Ba; but his very anonymity precludes any great reliance on his testimony.

For those who hold that it is as reasonable to conclude that the remains of the saint were buried as that they were burned, the question

The site of Becket's martyrdom in the north-west transept.

Detail of the murder of Thomas Becket; from the first known miniature of the martyrdom.

arises of whether the burial was done as an act of deception by the monks before the arrival of the Commissioners, or whether it was done by the Commissioners themselves in the execution either of their mandate or of their own discretion. The former was suggested by several commentators (including Routledge in 1895 and Moore in 1917) who pointed out that the monks were certainly capable of such an action. Bones and other relics were often moved from place to place,[4] and the monks' predecessors in the twelfth century had had no qualms about concealing the body of Becket to protect it from those who had killed him. Other monks elsewhere (in Ravenna and Durham) had probably done similar things. That the monks at Canterbury were not above a spot of deception is evidenced by their readiness to pass off another skull as that of Becket, and by their shameless pretence that the coloured water flowing from a spring to which they had added red ochre was the blood of the saint.

Nevertheless, it may be thought more likely that, if Becket's bones were really buried, it was done by the Commissioners. That is what happened elsewhere, and the monks would have been running an enormous risk in concocting a deliberate deception against the King and Cromwell. Moreover, there would have been no real need for them to do so unless they had grounds for believing that the relics would be burned or otherwise destroyed beyond redemption. But such grounds may not have existed. The monks of Christ Church would doubtless have heard from their Benedictine brethren that no such destructive act had been carried out against the remains of St Cuthbert at Durham, and may simply have assumed that a similar pattern would be followed in Canterbury. They may not even have cared very much, for the royal accounts show that they collaborated with the Commissioners in the destruction of the shrine, and were paid by the King for their labours.

For those who hold that the balance of the evidence points towards the burial of Becket's remains by the Commissioners rather than the monks, the question then arises of where the burial took place. There are some grounds for believing that it might have been beyond the walls of the Cathedral. Commissioners elsewhere were required to take the bones of unshrined saints, along with the riches of their shrines, to the Tower of London – though whether that was actually done is not clear. That Becket's bones might have been thus transported is hinted at in Thomas Derby's reference to a 'noble tower'.[5] Alternatively, they might have been interred in the monks' cemetery, as suggested in William Thomas's graphic phrase about their being 'spread amongst the bones of so many dead men'.[6] They might even, as Stanley suggested, have been mixed up with those of the other unshrined saints at Canterbury before being disposed of.[7] If this was indeed their fate, then, as William Thomas pointed out, they will never be found. If, on the other hand, the Commissioners were more likely to have buried the bones within the Cathedral, as they probably did elsewhere, where was the chosen site? In particular, was it associated in any way with the grave discovered in 1888?

There are several deeply puzzling features of the '1888 grave' and its contents that impressed people even before the second examination of the skeleton in 1949–51. The report of that examination merely deepened the mystery. In what circumstances could the skeleton of a body that had once been buried directly in the earth be dug up with great haste and carelessness, together with other bones and earthen debris, placed in a makeshift coffin with the skull mounted on a stone cushion and surround by the other bones, and buried a few inches beneath the surface in a place most intimately associated with St Thomas?

Although there are no direct reasons for believing the grave to be associated in any way with the treatment accorded to Becket's remains, the feeling persists that some kind of connection is possible. At the very least, the grave and its contents must be considered as highly unusual phenomena. Reading the clear and firm language of the Cave report, it is difficult to escape the conclusion that extraordinary processes were at work to produce the findings it recorded. Overwhelmingly, Professor Cave painted a picture of furtiveness, carelessness and haste in the exhumation of the body, probably from a communal grave site, yet of care in the way the bones were arranged within the makeshift coffin. This does not suggest a normal and straightforward burial; it smacks strongly of some kind of subterfuge. Moreover, the fact that the grave was not only unrecorded but even unknown until it was accidentally discovered in 1888 suggests that those who created it did not wish the site to be remembered or commemorated.

It is just such a consideration that points towards a tentative link with Becket, for if his remains had been buried discreetly by the Commissioners in 1538, then that site, too, would have been unmarked and uncommemorated. Not only that, it might well have been in the crypt, near to the place of his original burial. As several of the early commentators remarked (including those such as Father Morris who rejected the Becket hypothesis), the grave uncovered in 1888 gave every impression of being special, and the bones within it were thought by many to be of particular significance, even if they were not those of Becket himself.

Some may thus hold that the evidence supports the triple conclusions that Becket's bones were as likely to have been buried as burned in 1538, that the burial may have been done by the Commissioners with the intention of expunging the relics from the public consciousness, and that a connection may exist between the Commissioners' actions and the grave discovered in 1888. If so, then the 'solution' to the mystery of the grave in the eastern crypt must lie in the fifth hypothesis discussed in the preceding chapter. Two alternative possibilities were considered there. First, the Commissioners may have bestowed the true relics of Becket in that grave, where they still remain. They would not have been discovered in 1888 or 1949 because the Portland stone coffin was not removed on either occasion, leaving the ground beneath it undisturbed. According to this sequence of events, the '1888 coffin' with its baffling contents was inserted into the grave at a later date, for reasons that are simply unknowable. Secondly, the remains of Becket might originally have been laid by the Commissioners in the '1888 coffin', but removed at a later date by someone else and replaced by the hastily exhumed substitutes that came to light so dramatically in January 1888.

Choice between these twin alternatives is little more than guesswork; yet of the two, the latter seems, viscerally, to be the more likely. In this postulated sequence of events, the Commissioners secreted the bones of Becket in the '1888 coffin', being more concerned that they were simply out of the way than that they were interred in a fitting receptacle. The original site of Becket's tomb (in the next bay) would not have been available for the purpose, since the empty tomb itself would still have been standing there. The next most obvious choice of location in which to bury the remains might be the space immediately to the west of it – between the westernmost two of the three Purbeck marble pillars where the coffin was first discovered in 1888. The shallow depth of burial could be explained by a combination of the high level of the water table beneath the floor of the crypt and the fact that the Abbot of Evesham's coffin may already have been occupying the grave. At a later date the bones were removed from the coffin, reinterred elsewhere, and replaced by the '1888 skeleton' that was hastily and carelessly dug up from a common burial site and arranged in the coffin to give the impression, should any subsequent enquiry be made, that the bones were those of the saint.

Why this was done, when, and by whom, are questions upon which the evidence throws no light at all. A possible time would be in, or shortly after, 1546, when the eastern crypt was walled off for the personal use of the first prebendary, Richard Thornden. Thornden was a former monk of the Priory of Christ Church who remained sympathetic to the Catholic cause and who might have preferred to see the saint's remains interred in the church rather than in his faggot cellar. Alternatively, it might have been done during the Puritan purge of the Cathedral in 1643, when many tombs in the nave were opened and their contents removed. Whether the destructive energies of the new Commissioners of Cromwell (this time, Oliver rather than Thomas) extended to the walled-off eastern crypt is not known; but the fear of such penetration could have been sufficient to persuade those who knew its secret to remove the bones for safer keeping elsewhere.

That this may not be a wholly idiosyncratic account of the events that followed the destruction of the shrine in 1538 is suggested by the one piece of the mystery that remains to be put into its place in this web of possibilities: whether there are (or have been) any conspiracies about the truth of Becket's bones. Two have been intimated in the preceding chapters. The first was the allegation, made pseudonymously by 'Thomas Chough' in 1990, of the existence of a coterie of people who are party to the secret of the true resting place of Becket's relics and who pray there twice a year for the conversion of England. The allegation appears to be true in that a small group of those who believe in the continued existence of the relics do gather at the site twice a year. While their belief *may* be based on clear historical evidence that has never been made public, this is rather unlikely.

A second possible conspiracy surrounds the actions of Canon John Shirley and Archdeacon Julian Bickersteth in the 1950s in instigating and personally contributing to the refurbishment of the Chapels of St Mary Magdalene and St Nicholas, in the north crypt transept, as soon as the Cave report had shown that the '1888 skeleton' was not that of Becket. Did they discover something about the two graves in these chapels that led them to secure the Chapter's agreement to the reopening of the '1888 grave' in 1949, and then, following the confirmation of the Cave report in 1951, to direct their attention away from the eastern crypt towards the north transept? Tempting though it may be to advance an affirmative answer, there would be no foundation for it in the evidence. There are certainly several curiosities in the sequence of events, but nothing to confirm any special or secret knowledge they may have acquired between about 1948 and 1951.

Nevertheless, the actions of Shirley and Bickersteth in refurbishing these chapels, and Shirley's choice of St Mary Magdalene for his own final resting place, may not be unconnected with the mystery of Becket's bones. Both men would have read the Cave report in 1951 with great care, and neither is likely simply to have put it aside and drawn the episode of the skeleton in the eastern crypt to an uncritical close. They can scarcely have missed the extraordinary findings, which Cave almost went out of his way to emphasise, about the animal bones in the coffin, about the previous burial of the skeleton directly in earth, and about the hasty carelessness with which it had been exhumed; and they must surely have pondered their significance. Armed with Professor Cave's conclusions and the welter of other historical material that would readily have been available to them, they may possibly have travelled down the same path that this chapter has attempted to follow, perhaps arriving at the same conclusion. They, too, might have ended up suspecting that the '1888 coffin' had once contained the true bones of Becket, only for them to have been removed at a later date and replaced by others that had been hastily exhumed from elsewhere.

If so, then Shirley and Bickersteth would finally have had to face the ultimate question: whither were the bones taken and reinterred? In answering it, they would have drawn upon their own beliefs and understandings about the true fate of the saint's relics. Could it have been through this route that they were led to the graves in what are now the two beautifully restored Norman Chapels of St Mary Magdalene and St Nicholas, there to pay their personal, discreet respects to the most celebrated of all the English saints? If so, they would not have been alone – for it is precisely there, where burns the red lamp of martyrdom, that they would have encountered 'Thomas Chough's' small group of believers.

Becket's martyrdom embroidered on a mitre; English, 1180–1200.

Notes

Prologue: Raiders in the Night

1 *Kentish Gazette*, 24 August 1990.
2 *Ibid.*
3 *Kentish Gazette*, 7 September 1990.

1 In Life and in Death

1 There are many biographies of the life and death of Becket. The most recent, upon which this chapter draws in parts, is F. Barlow, *Thomas Becket*, London, 1986.
2 G. Greenaway, *The Life and Death of Thomas Becket, Chancellor of England and Archbishop of Canterbury, based on the Account of William fitzStephen, his Clerk*, London, 1961.
3 W. Stubbs (ed), *The Historical Works of Gervase of Canterbury*, Volumes I and II. London, 1879 and 1880. For Benedict see J.C. Robertson, *Materials for the History of Thomas Becket*, Volume II. London, 1876.
4 W.A. Scott Robertson, 'The Crypt of Canterbury Cathedral', *Archaeologia Cantiana*, XIII, 1880, p.53.
5 There are many accounts of the history of Canterbury Cathedral. Much of the material in the remainder of this chapter is taken from R. Willis, *The Architectural History of Canterbury Cathedral*, London, 1845, and C.E. Woodruff, and W. Danks, *Memorials of the Cathedral and Priory of Christ in Canterbury*, London, 1912.
6 A.J. Mason, *What Became of the Bones of St Thomas?*, Cambridge, 1920, pp. 98–9.
7 Quoted *ibid.*, pp. 71–2.

8 Barlow, *op. cit.*, p. 8.
9 *Ibid.*
10 T. Tatton-Brown, 'The Trinity Chapel and Corona Floors', *Canterbury Cathedral Chronicle*, 75, 1981, pp. 51–5.
11 The drawing is reproduced in A.P. Stanley, *Historical Memorials of Canterbury*, London, 1912 (11th edition), facing p. 291, and in R. Strong, *Lost Treasures of Britain*, London, 1990, p. 28.
12 D. Erasmus, *Pilgrimages to St Mary of Walsingham and St Thomas of Canterbury*, trans. J.G. Nichols, Westminster, 1849, pp. 44–60.
13 *Ibid*, p. 55.
14 Stanley, *op. cit.*, p. 288.
15 *Ibid.*, p. 291.
16 Erasmus, *op. cit.*
17 Strong, *op. cit.*, pp. 19–20.
18 Stanley, *op. cit.*, p. 243.

2 The Skeleton in the Crypt

1 C.F. Routledge, J.B. Sheppard and W.A. Scott Robertson, 'The Crypt of Canterbury Cathedral', *Archaeologia Cantiana*, XVIII, 1889, pp. 253–6.
2 W.P. Thornton, 'Surgical Report on a Skeleton Found in the Crypt of Canterbury Cathedral', *Archaeologia Cantiana*, XVIII, 1889, pp. 257–60.
3 A.J. Mason, *What Became of the Bones of St Thomas?*, Cambridge, 1920, p. 183.
4 Routledge *et al*, *op. cit.*, p. 255.
5 J. Morris, letter to *The Times*, 20 February 1888.
6 Mason, *op. cit.*, p. 181.
7 W.P. Thornton, *Becket's Bones*, Canterbury, 1901, p. 4.

8   Mason, *op. cit.*, p. 174.
9   Thornton, 1901, *op. cit.*, p. 5.
10 Mason, *op. cit.*, p. 178.
11 Thornton, 1901, *op. cit.*, p. 5.
12 Mason, *op. cit.*, pp. 175–82.
13 *Ibid.*
14 *Ibid.*, p. 182.
15 W.P. Thornton, letter to *The Times*, 16 February 1888.
16 Thornton, 1889, *op. cit.*
17 Thornton, 1901, *op. cit.*
18 Thornton, 1901, *op. cit.*, pp. 7–8.
19 Anon., *Proceedings of the Society of Antiquaries*, 5 December 1907, p. 13.
20 Mason, *op. cit.*, p. 179.
21 Thornton, 1901, *op. cit.*, p. 6.
22 Anon., letter to *The Times*, 20 February 1888.
23 H.G. Austin, letter to *The Times*, 15 February 1888.
24 Mason, *op. cit.*, pp. 179–80.

3   Believers, Agnostics and Sceptics

1   O. Chadwick, *The Victorian Church, Part II*, London, 1972, p. 352.
2   *Ibid.*, pp. 406–7.
3   *Ibid.*, pp. 353–4.
4   *Ibid.*, p. 367.
5   C.E. Woodruff and W. Danks, *Memorials of the Cathedral and Priory of Christ in Canterbury*, London, 1912, pp. 364–5.
6   A.J. Mason, *What Became of the Bones of St Thomas?*, Cambridge, 1920, p. 189.
7   T. Borenius, *St Thomas Becket in Art*, London, 1932.
8   C.F. Routledge, J.B. Sheppard and A.W. Scott Robertson, 'The Crypt of Canterbury Cathedral', *Archaeologia Cantiana*, XVIII, 1889, p. 255.
9   Quoted in M. Beazeley, *The Canterbury Bones*, London, 1913, pp. 5–6.
10 *Ibid.*
11 *Ibid.*
12 J. Morris, letter to *The Times*, 10 February 1888.
13 *Minutes of the Canterbury Chapter*, 25 November 1887.
14 Mason, *op. cit.*, p. 176.
15 *Ibid.*, p. 177.
16 *Ibid.*, p. 176.
17 H.G. Austin, letter to *The Times*, 15 February 1888.
18 C.F. Routledge, letter to *The Times*, 15 February 1888.
19 C.F. Routledge, 'The Bones of Archbishop Becket', *Archaeologia Cantiana*, XXI, 1895, pp. 73–80.
20 *Ibid.*, p. 80.
21 W.P. Thornton, 'Surgical Report of a Skeleton Found in the Crypt of Canterbury Cathedral', *Archaeologia Cantiana*, XVIII, 1889, p. 260.
22 W.P. Thornton, letter to *The Times*, 16 February 1888.
23 W.P. Thornton, letter to *The Times*, 9 March 1888.
24 W.P. Thornton, *Becket's Bones*, Canterbury, 1901, pp. 10–11.
25 Quoted in Mason, *op. cit.*, p. 177.
26 *Ibid.*, p. 178.
27 *Ibid.*, p. 181.
28 Routledge *et al.*, *op. cit.*, p. 256.
29 *Minutes of the Canterbury Chapter*, 19 May 1888.
30 *Minutes of the Canterbury Chapter*, 30 July 1888.
31 Mason, *op. cit.*, pp. 176 and 178.
32 E. Venables, letter to *The Times*, 16 March 1888.
33 Morris, *op. cit.*
34 Thornton, 1901, *op. cit.*, p. 6.
35 Morris, *op. cit.*
36 J. Morris, letter to *The Times*, 20 February 1888. J. Morris, letter to *The Times*, 28 February 1888; Austin, *op. cit.*; Routledge, 1888, *op. cit.*; Thornton, 16 February 1888, *op. cit.*
37 E.V. Hitchcock, (ed.) *The Life and Death of Sr Thomas Moore, Knight, Sometime Lord High Chancellor of England, Written in the Tyme of Queene Marie by Nicholas Harpsfield*, Oxford, 1932.
38 A.P. Stanley, *Historical Memorials of Canterbury*, London, 1912 (11th edition), p. 244n.
39 Morris, 28 February 1888, *op. cit.*
40 J. Morris, letter to *The Times*, 16 March 1888.
41 Thornton, 9 March 1888, *op. cit.*

4   *Debating the Bones*

1   Quoted in W. Hutton, *Thomas Becket, Archbishop of Canterbury*, Cambridge, 1926, p. 284.
2   Quoted in Canterbury Cathedral Archives, Add. MS 313.
3   H.S. Milman, 'The Vanished Memorials of St Thomas of Canterbury', *Archaeologia*, Second Series, LIII, 1892, pp. 211–28.
4   *Ibid.*, p. 211.
5   *Ibid.*, p. 221.
6   Quoted in Milman, *op. cit.*, p. 221.
7   Quoted *ibid.*, p. 223.
8   *Ibid.*, p. 224.
9   C.F. Routledge, 'The Bones of Archbishop Becket', *Archaeologia Cantiana*, XXI, 1895, pp. 73–80.
10   *Ibid.*, p. 77.
11   J. Morris, letter to *The Times*, 20 February 1888.
12   W.P. Thornton, *Becket's Bones*, Canterbury, 1901.
13   W.P. Thornton, 'Surgical Report of a Skeleton Found in the Crypt of Canterbury Cathedral', *Archaeologia Cantiana*, XVIII, 1889, p. 260.
14   M. Beazeley, 'On Certain Human Remains Found in the Crypt of Canterbury Cathedral and Supposed by Some to be Those of Archbishop Becket', *Proceedings of the Society of Antiquaries*, 5 December 1907, pp. 1–14.
15   M. Beazeley, *The Canterbury Bones*, London, 1913.
16   *Ibid.*, p. 9.
17   A.J. Mason, *What Became of the Bones of St Thomas?*, Cambridge, 1920, p. 189.
18   Beazeley, 1913, *op. cit.*, p. 13.
19   J.H. Pollen, 'Becket's Bones', *Month*, CXI, 1908, pp. 87–90.
20   Beazeley, 1913, *op. cit.*, p. 23.
21   *Ibid.*, p. 36.
22   Beazeley, 1907, *op. cit.*, pp. 12–14.
23   C.E. Woodruff and W. Danks, *Memorials of the Cathedral and Priory of Christ in Canterbury*, London, 1912, p. 82.
24   *Ibid.*
25   C.E. Woodruff, 'The Cult of St Thomas of Canterbury', *Archaeologia Cantiana*, XLIV, 1932, pp. 13–32.
26   E. Moore, *Studies in Dante. Fourth Series. Textual Criticism of the Convivio and Miscellaneous Essays*, New York, 1968 (first published 1917).
27   Quoted *ibid.*, p. 191.
28   W. Page, (ed.) *The Victoria History of the County of Durham*, London, 1905.
29   Mason, *op. cit.*, p. 129.
30   Moore, *op. cit.*, p. 198.
31   *Ibid.*
32   Beazeley, 1913, *op. cit.*
33   Moore, *op. cit.*, p. 202.
34   Routledge, *op. cit.*, p. 77.
35   W.H. Hutton, *St Thomas of Canterbury*, London, 1889, p. 175.
36   Moore, *op. cit.*, p. 205.
37   *Ibid.*, pp. 205–6.
38   E. Duffy, *The Stripping of the Altars*, London and New Haven, 1992, pp. 525–6.
39   Moore, *op. cit.*, p. 206.
40   *Ibid.*, p. 208.

5   *Archiepiscopal Intervention*

1   D.L. Edwards, *Leaders of the Church of England, 1828–1944*, London, 1971, p. 249.
2   A.R. Vidler, *The Church in an Age of Revolution: 1789 to the Present Day*, London, 1971, p. 163.
3   J.W.C. Wand, *Anglicanism in History and Today*, London, 1961, p. 143.
4   Vidler, *op. cit.*, p. 166.
5   A.J. Mason, *What Became of the Bones of St Thomas?*, Cambridge, 1920, p. 187.
6   *Ibid.*
7   W.H. Hutton, *Thomas Becket, Archbishop of Canterbury*, Cambridge, 1926, p. 299.
8   *Ibid.*, p. 305.
9   F. Barlow, *Thomas Becket*, London, 1986.
10   Quoted in Mason, *op. cit.*, p. 37.
11   *Ibid.*, p. 50.
12   *Ibid.*, p. 53.
13   *Ibid.*, p. 55.
14   *Ibid.*, p. 55.

15 *Ibid.*, p. 185.
16 D.I. Hill, *Christ's Glorious Church: the Story of Canterbury Cathedral*, London, 1976, p.49.
17 Mason, *op. cit.*, p. 187.
18 *Ibid.*, p. 191.
19 *Ibid.*, p. 193.

6   *The Grave Revisited*

1   Canterbury Cathedral Archives, Add. MS 313.
2   A.J.E. Cave, *Report to the Dean and Chapter of Canterbury Cathedral on a Skeleton Buried in the Cathedral Crypt*, 1951, unpublished MS, Canterbury Cathedral Library, p. 1.
3   *Minutes of the Canterbury Chapter*, 5 February 1949.
4   D.L. Edwards, *F.J. Shirley. An Extraordinary Headmaster*, London, 1969.
5   *Ibid.*, p. 81.
6   F.J. Shirley, 'Scientists' Examination of Canterbury Bones', *The Times*, 4 August 1951. See also F.J. Shirley, 'Ancient Human Bones from Canterbury Cathedral', *Archaeologia Cantiana*, LXIV, 1951, pp. 112–15.
7   *Minutes of the Canterbury Chapter*, 12 October 1946.
8   *Ibid.*, 26 October 1946.
9   *Ibid.*, 2 November 1946.
10 *Ibid.*, 22 May 1948.
11 *Ibid.*, 4 June 1948.
12 *Ibid.*, 18 September 1948.
13 *Ibid.*, 2 October 1948.
14 *Ibid.*, 22 October 1949.
15 Shirley, *op. cit.*, *The Times*.
16 *Minutes of the Canterbury Chapter*, 23 June 1951.
17 *Ibid.*, 22 September 1951.
18 Shirley, *op. cit.*, *The Times*.
19 Canterbury Cathedral Archives, Add. MS 313.
20 Cave, *op. cit.*, p.8.
21 *Ibid.*, p. 9.
22 *Ibid.*, p. 10.
23 *Ibid.*, p. 29.
24 C.F. Routledge, J.B. Sheppard and W.A. Scott Robertson, 'The Crypt of Canterbury Cathedral', *Archaeologia Cantiana*, XVIII, 1889, pp. 253–6.
25 W.P. Thornton, *Becket's Bones*, Canterbury, 1901, p. 3.
26 A.J. Mason, *What Became of the Bones of St Thomas?*, Cambridge, 1920, p. 183.
27 Cave, *op. cit.*, pp. 27 and 29.
28 *Ibid.*, pp. 24 and 27.
29 *Ibid.*, p. 30.
30 *Minutes of the Canterbury Chapter*, 23 June 1951.
31 G. Gustafson, 'Age of Determination of Teeth', *Journal of the American Dental Association*, 41, 1951, p. 45.

7   *Burned or Buried?*

1   J.M.C. Crum, letter to *The Times*, 13 August 1951.
2   M. Sparks, *Canterbury Cathedral Chronicle*, 86, 1992, pp. 36–7.
3   L. Lang-Sims, 'Sarsnet and Old Bones', *Canterbury Cathedral Chronicle*, 75, 1981, pp. 34–8.
4   J. Bentley, *Restless Bones*, London, 1985.
5   D. Sox, *Relics and Shrines*, London, 1985.
6   M.D. Anthony, *The Becket Factor*, London, 1990.
7   A.P. Stanley, *Historical Memorials of Canterbury*, London, 1912, (11th edition), p. 243.
8   G.H. Cook, *Letters to Cromwell and Others on the Suppression of the Monasteries*, London, 1965, p. 5.
9   *Ibid.*, p. 57.
10 *Ibid.*, p. 58.
11 H. Thurston and D. Attwater, *The Lives of the Saints*, London, 1956, pt IV, p. 637.
12 A.J. Mason, *What Became of the Bones of St Thomas?*, Cambridge, 1920, p. 123.
13 J. Gairdner, (ed.) *Letters and Papers, Foreign and Domestic, on the Reign of Henry VIII*, London, 1893, XVI, 1233, 1262.
14 H.S. Milman, 'The Vanished Memorials of St Thomas of Canterbury', *Archaeologia*, Second Series, LIII, 1892, p. 219.

15 *Letters and Papers, op. cit.*, XIII, pt II, 1049.

16 *Ibid.*, 1103.

17 *Ibid.*, 1280 (40b).

18 *Ibid.*, XV, 772.

19 *Ibid.*, XIII, pt II, 401.

20 *Ibid.*, XIII, pt II, 442.

21 Mason, *op. cit.*, p. 130.

22 Stanley, *op. cit.*, p. 244.

23 *Letters and Papers, op. cit.*, XIII, pt II, 848.

24 *Ibid.*, XIII, pt II, 133, 134.

25 *Ibid.*, XIII, pt II, 257.

26 W.D. Hamilton, *A Chronicle of England During the Reign of the Tudors from AD 1485 to 1559 by Charles Wriothesley, Windsor Herald*, London (Camden Society), 1875, p. 87n.

27 Letters and Papers, *op. cit.*, XIII, pt II, 684.

28 *Ibid.*, 1087.

29 Quoted in Mason, *op. cit.*, p. 132.

30 *Letters and Papers, op. cit.*, XIII, pt II, 542.

31 *Ibid.*, 974.

32 *Ibid.*, XIV, pt I, 11.

33 *Ibid.*, XIII, pt II, 880.

34 *Ibid.*, XIV, pt I, 200.

35 *Ibid.*, 536.

36 G. Constant, *The Reformation in England. 1 The English Schism*, London, 1934, pp. 443 and 453–4.

37 G. Townsend, *The Acts and Monuments of John Foxe*, London, 1843, pp. 187–202.

38 W. Urry, Unpublished and undated MS on the life of Thomas Becket. Reproduced by kind permission of Mrs K. Urry.

39 Townsend, *op. cit.*, p. 202.

40 E.V. Hitchcock, (ed.) *The Life and Death of Sr Thomas Moore, Knight, Sometime Lord High Chancellor of England, Written in the Tyme of Queene Marie by Nicholas Harpsfield*, Oxford, 1932.

41 Quoted in Mason, *op. cit.*, p. 139. See also Hitchcock, *op. cit.*, p. 215.

42 Mason, *op. cit.*, p. 139ff.

43 C. Wordsworth, *Ecclesiastical Biography or Lives of Eminent Men Connected with the History of Religion in England from the Commencement of the Reformation to the Revolution*, London, 1818, (2nd Edition), vol II.

44 *Ibid.*, p. 55n.

45 Quoted in Milman, *op. cit.*, p. 226.

46 Hitchcock, *op. cit.*, p. 215, emphasis added.

47 Wordsworth, *op. cit.*, p. 226, emphasis added.

48 *Ibid.*, p. 56.

49 Mason, *op. cit.*, p. 148.

50 Hamilton, *op. cit.*, p. 86.

51 *Ibid.*, pp. 86–7.

52 D. Erasmus, *Pilgrimages to St Mary of Walsingham and St Thomas of Canterbury*, trans. J.G. Nichols, Westminster, 1849, p. 47.

53 Hamilton, *op. cit.*, p. 87n.

54 Quoted in Milman, *op. cit.*, p. 227.

55 *Letters and Papers, op. cit.*, XIV, pt I, 402.

56 Milman, *op. cit.*, p. 222.

57 Mason, *op. cit.*, p. 159n.

58 M. Beazeley, *The Canterbury Bones*, London, 1913, pp. 33–4.

59 Quoted in Mason, *op. cit.*, p. 160.

60 *Ibid.*, p. 162.

61 *Ibid.*, pp. 162–3.

62 *Letters and Papers, op. cit.*, XIII, pt II, 1280.

63 C.F. Routledge, 'The Bones of Archbishop Becket', *Archaeologia Cantiana*, XXI, 1895, pp. 73–80; E. Moore, *Studies in Dante. Fourth Series. Textual Criticism of the Convivio and Miscellaneous Essays*, New York, 1968 (first published in 1917).

64 Bentley, *op. cit.*

65 W. Urry, 'Some Notes on the Two Resting Places of St Thomas Becket at Canterbury', *Thomas Becket, Actes du Colloque International de Sedièvres*, ed. R. Foreville, Sedièvres, 1975, pp. 195–209.

8   *Five Hypotheses*

1 M. Beazeley, *The Canterbury Bones*, London, 1913.

2 A.J. Mason, *What Became of the Bones of St Thomas?*, Cambridge, 1920, p. 193.

3 C.E. Woodruff, and W. Danks, *Memorials of the Cathedral and Priory of Christ in Canterbury*, London, 1912, p. 14.
4 *Ibid.*, p. 281.
5 *Ibid.*, p. 282–3.
6 *Ibid.*, p. 94.
7 Mason, *op. cit.*, p. 176n.
8 J. Morris, letter to *The Times*, 20 February 1888.
9 Mason, *op. cit.*, p. 176.
10 Morris, *op. cit.*
11 H.S. Milman, 'The Vanished Memorials of St Thomas of Canterbury', *Archaeologia*, Second Series, LIII, 1892, pp. 211–28.
12 Quoted *ibid.*, p. 223.
13 D.I. Hill, *Canterbury Cathedral*, London, 1986, p. 61.
14 T. Hay, 'The Ledger Slabs of Canterbury Cathedral 1991', *Archaeologia Cantiana*, CIX, 1991, pp. 5–15.
15 W. Somner and N. Battley, *The Antiquities of Canterbury*, London, 1703, Part II, p. 35.
16 D. Sox, *Relics and Shrines*, London, 1985, p. 74.
17 T. Chough, letter to the *Kentish Gazette*, 7 September 1990.
18 D.L. Edwards, *F.J. Shirley, An Extraordinary Headmaster*, London, 1969, p. 77.
19 F.J. Shirley, 'Scientists' Examination of the Canterbury Bones', *The Times*, 4 August 1951.
20 Sox, *op. cit.*, p. 74.
21 Edwards, *op. cit.*, pp. 84–5.
22 *Ibid.*, p. 84.
23 *Minutes of the Canterbury Chapter*, 23 June 1951.
24 *Ibid.*, 14 July 1951.
25 *Ibid.*, 5 February 1949.
26 J. Gairdner, (ed.) *Letters and Papers, Foreign and Domestic, on the Reign of Henry VIII*, London, 1893, XVI, 1233, 1262.
27 Beazeley, *op. cit.*
28 Mason, *op. cit.*, p. 183.

9 *A Mystery*

1 G. Townsend, *The Acts and Monuments of John Foxe*, London, 1843, p. 204.
2 E.V. Hitchcock, (ed.) *The Life and Death of Sr Thomas Moore, Knight, Sometime Lord High Chancellor of England, Written in the Tyme of Queene Marie by Nicholas Harpsfield*, Oxford, 1932, p. 215.
3 A.J. Mason, *What Became of the Bones of St Thomas?*, Cambridge, 1920, p. 140.
4 J. Bentley, *Restless Bones*, London, 1985.
5 J. Gairdner, (ed.) *Letters and Papers, Foreign and Domestic, on the Reign of Henry VIII*, London, 1893, XIV, pt I, 402.
6 Quoted in Mason, *op. cit.*, pp. 162–3.
7 A.P. Stanley, *Historical Memorials of Canterbury*, London, 1912, (11th Edition), p. 244.

Index

Aberdeen, University of, 144
Aelfric, Archbishop of Canterbury, 137
Aelthelgar, Archbishop of Canterbury, 137
Aethelm, Archbishop of Canterbury, 137
Alan of Tewkesbury, 42
Altar of the Trinity (Trinity Chapel), 23
Anglo-Catholicism, 43, 78
Annals (of John Stow), 126
Antiquities of Canterbury (1703), 144
Antonio Santi, Fra, 70
Archaeologia, 58
Archaeologia Cantiana, 35, 100
Archbishop of Cologne, 20
Archbishop of Lyons, 20
Archbishop of Rheims, 20
Archbishop's Palace, the, 6
Archdeacon of Canterbury (1949), 95
Arkasden, 58, 64, 77, 132
Audeville, William de, Abbot of Evesham,
    66, 73, 75, 100, 136, 152–3, 155, 167
Austin, H.G., 37, 40–41, 49, 53, 55, 77, 132

Balfour, Arthur James, 78
Barlow, Frank, Professor, 4
Beadle, Mr G.B., 98
Beazeley, Mr M. (Hon. Librarian to Dean
    and Chapter of Canterbury), 64–7, 73,
    77, 125, 129, 132, 136, 152
Becket, St Thomas (St Thomas of
    Canterbury), 33, 42, 54, 66, 71, 76, 78,
    83–4, 86, 93, 96, 98, 102, 106, 108, 117–20,
    122, 130–31, 138–9, 143, 150–54, 156–7,
    161, 166
        age of at death, 48, 103; appointed
        Archdeacon of Canterbury, 1;
        appointed Chancellor, 1; approxi-
        mate date of birth of, 48; biographies
        of, 23, 25; birth of, 1; burial of, ix, 14,
        90; canonised, 17; consecrated
        Archbishop, 1; cult of, 31, 68; design
        for 'tomb' of (1948), 98–9, 162; final
        hours of, 84; first tomb of, 16–17,
        19–20, 23, 25, 63, 139, 153, 160, 167;
        'head'/purported skull of, 31, 90,
        119, 125–6, 128–9, 143, 162, 165;
        height of, 65; images of, 118; life of,
        1f.; linen tunic belonging to, 157–8;

memorials of, 58, 156; miraculous
    powers of, 16, 84; murder of, 8, 13,
    54–7, 75, 83–4, 86, 87, 89, 92, 102–3,
    123, 126, 133, 144, 156–7, 169; parents
    of, 1; remains of, ix–xii, 13, 16, 20, 23,
    27, 33, 35, 44–6, 48–52, 55–60, 63–7,
    69, 73, 75–6, 78, 80, 82, 89–90, 92, 93,
    99, 101–2, 107, 109–10, 116–17,
    119–33, 135, 139–41, 143–4, 148–54,
    156–62, 165–9; remains translated,
    20, 23, 126, 159; resigns Chancellor-
    ship, 1; shrine of, ix–xi, 20, 23, 30–31,
    35, 59, 63, 75, 93, 111–12, 118, 121,
    124–7, 130–31, 135, 139, 141; 'Trial'
    of, 118–20
'Becket Hypothesis', the, 53, 64, 68, 75, 77,
    103, 105, 109, 138, 156, 166
Becket Leaves, the, 3, 6, 77
Becket's Bones (title of pamphlet by
    Thornton), 38, 64
Benedict of Peterborough, monk of Christ
    Church Priory, 14, 16, 83–4, 87, 89–90
Benson, Edward White, Archbishop of
    Canterbury, 44, 80
Bentley, James, 109
Bertrand de Poyet, Cardinal, 70
Bickersteth, Ella, 148
Bickersteth, Julian, Archdeacon of
    Maidstone, xi, 95, 144, 147–9, 168–9
Bickersteth, Rev Dr Samuel, 144, 148
Bishop of London (at time of Becket), 3
Bishop of Salisbury (at time of Becket), 3
Black Prince, the, 141
Bodleian Library, the, 130
Bodley, G.F., 43
Book of Common Prayer, the, 78, 80, 82
Bregwyn, Archbishop of Canterbury, 137
Breton, Richard le, 4, 13, 86
British Academy, the, 69, 97
British Library, the, 25
British Museum, the, 55–6, 123, 130
Broc, Randolph de, 4, 13–14

Calendar of State Papers, the, 65
Cambridge, University of, 50, 80, 82, 95–6, 107
Canterbury, 33, 51, 66, 70, 72, 76, 82, 86, 100,
    106, 111, 115, 117, 120, 122–3, 130, 132,

140, 144, 148, 150, 156, 162, 165
  Becket's arrival in, 3; Becket's assassins arrival in, 4; Burgate Street, 17; Cross of, 109; Henry VIII in, 65; houses in, 20; townspeople mourn Becket, 13; pilgrimage to, ix, 31, 46, 127, 156–7; suppression of Monasteries in, 32; unshrined saints of, 60
Canterbury Bones, The, 64, 129, 136
Canterbury Cathedral, ix–xi, 3, 17, 23, 25, 33, 44, 53, 55, 58, 60, 67, 69, 80, 82–3, 90, 97, 112, 114, 116, 119, 126, 131, 136, 138, 143–4, 148, 156–7, 159, 162, 166
  Archives of, 95, 100, 107, 132; Archivist of, xi; Becket seeks sanctuary in, 13; Chapel of St Benedict (*see also* St Benedict, Altar of), 4, 8; Chapel of St Mary Magdalene (*see also* St Mary Magdalene, Altar of), xi, 109, 117, 143–4, 147–8, 168–9; Chapel of St Nicholas, xi, 143, 147–8, 168–9; Chapel of the Holy Trinity, eastern crypt, 14, 16, 19, 158; Chapter House, 3, 4; choir of, 17, 23; cloisters, 4; crypt, xi–xii, 14, 16–19, 25, 66, 73, 109, 139, 152–4, 158, 166; (Dean and) Chapter of, x, 35, 37, 41, 48, 51–2, 64, 93, 96–101, 104, 132–3, 147–50, 160, 162, 168; earlier Norman building, 35; eastern crypt, 19–20, 23, 31, 35, 43, 46, 58, 68–9, 76, 91–2, 95, 98–9, 107, 109, 122, 132–3, 136–7, 139, 147–51, 153–4, 156, 158, 160–62, 167–8; excavations in, 35, 52, 153, 155, 160; high altar of, 4, 8, 158; Jesus Chapel, 69; Library of, 96, 99–100, 107, 132; 'Miracle Windows', Trinity Chapel, 17, 25, 27; north choir aisle of, 25; north crypt transept of, 117, 143–4, 149, 168; north-west transept of, 4; Our Lady in the Undercroft, altar of, xi, 16, 18, 73, 75, 132; plan of, 9; precincts of, ix, 109, 140, 153; 'Puritan Purge' of (1643), 167–8; Receiver General of, 100; reconstructed after fire, 17–18, 20; St Augustine of Canterbury, altar of, 14; St Augustine's Chair, 4; St Benedict, altar of, 8; St Gabriel's Chapel, 16; St John the Baptist, altar of, 14; St Mary Magdalene, altar of, xi, 144; St Michael's Chapel, xi; staff of, 40; treasurer of, xi, 147; Trinity Chapel, ix–x, 17–18, 25, 27, 31, 35, 45, 60, 63, 65, 73, 75, 79, 90, 105, 128, 135, 141, 159; western crypt, 18
Canterbury Cathedral Chronicle, The, 109
Canute, King, 136
Castelnau, Bishop of Tarbes, 119

Catherine of Aragon, Queen, 123
Cave, Prof A.J.E., 95–6, 99–106, 110, 136–7, 147, 149, 153, 166, 168–9
Cave Report, the, 99–101, 103–4, 107, 109–10, 133, 139, 147, 150, 166, 168
Charles V, Emperor, 120
Chartres, Dean of, 20
Chaucer, Geoffrey, 156
Cheapside, London, 1
Chichester (Cathedral), 90, 114–15, 117, 122
Chough, Thomas, x, 144, 168–9
Christ Church, Oxford, 144, 147
Chronicle (Holinshed), 126
Chronicle (Wriothesley), 126–7
Chronicles of the Abbots of Evesham, the, 66, 152
Church Association, the, 44
Church of Burlingham St Andrew, Norfolk, 118
Church of England, the, 43–4, 78–80, 82, 91, 109
Church of St Dunstan, 17
Church of SS. Giovanni e Paolo, Spoleto, 11
Church of the Frati Minori, the, Ravenna, 69–70
Church, Dr R.W., Dean of St Paul's, 43
Colet, John, Dean of St Paul's, 31–2, 126
College of St Beuno, North Wales, 53
College of Six Preachers, the, 117
Constable of France, the, 122
Constitutions of Clarendon, the, 1
Contributions to the Textual Criticism of the Divina Commedia, 69
Convocations of Canterbury and York, the, 78
Cottonian Manuscript, British Library, 25, 27, 46
Court of Brussels, the, 120
Courtenay, William, Archbishop of Canterbury (1381–96), 141
Cranmer, Archbishop Thomas, 114, 151–2
Cromwell, Oliver, 168
Cromwell, Thomas, Lord Privy Seal, 32, 52, 65–6, 112, 114–15, 117, 119–20, 122, 125–7, 130–33, 159, 162, 165

Danks, Canon William, Canon Residentiary, Canterbury, 67
Dante Alighieri, 68–71, 73, 76
Davidson, Randall Thomas, Archbishop of Canterbury, 78–80, 160
Derby, Thomas, Clerk to the Privy Council, 59–60, 93, 127, 130, 141, 165
Durham, 71–3, 76, 90, 117, 132, 151, 157, 165
Durham Cathedral, 71–3, 116–17
Durham Cathedral, Dean and Chapter of, 72

Ecclesiastical Biography (Wordsworth), 123–4

Ecclesiastical Commissioners, the, 44
Edward IV, King, 144
Edward the Confessor, King (St Edward
    the Confessor), 76, 92, 119, 157
Edwards, Very Rev David L., 147
1888 remains, the, xii, 35–8, 40–6, 48–58, 60,
    63–8, 73, 75, 78, 83, 89–90, 92–3, 96, 98,
    101–7, 109–10, 133, 135–9, 147, 149–50,
    152–6, 159–62, 166–8
Elizabeth, Queen, Consort of Edward IV,
    144
Elizabeth I, Queen, x, 125
Elyas of Dereham, 25
Emden, Alfred (A.B.), 69, 96–7, 99, 147–8
English College, Rome, 53
Erasmus, Desiderius, 25–6, 31–2, 126
Ernold the Goldsmith, Monk of
    Canterbury, 14
Eton College, 50

Faith-Craft Works Ltd, 98
Felsted School, Essex, 147
56th Territorial Division, the 147
First Epistle of St Peter, the, 127
First World War, the, 78, 82
Fisher, St John, 53
fitzStephen, William, 8, 14, 48, 54, 83–4, 87
fitzUrse, Reginald, 4, 83–4, 86, 89

Gardiner, Rev R.B., 67
Gardiner, Stephen, Bishop of Winchester,
    116
Garnier de Pont-Sainte Maxence, 84, 86–7
Gaspard de Coligny, ix
General Medical Council, Medical Register
    of, 51
Gervase, Monk of Priory of Christ Church,
    Canterbury, 14, 16, 84, 86–7, 89–90, 92,
    103
Gloucester Cathedral, 44
Grim, Edward, 11, 13, 83–4, 86–7, 89, 144
Gustafson, Dr Gosta, 107

Hall, Dr Hamilton, 67
Hampton Court, 114
Harpsfield, Nicholas, Archdeacon of
    Canterbury, 55–6, 63, 65, 122–5, 159, 162
Harrow School, 53
Hart House, University of Toronto, 144
Hastings Hours, the, 46
Hennage, Dr George, 115
Henry II, King, 1, 3–4, 17, 20, 33, 155
Henry III, King, 1, 20, 23
Henry IV, King, 29, 141
Henry VIII, King, 33, 48, 59, 65–7, 72, 76, 90,
    92, 114, 116–23, 125–6, 129–32, 151–2,
    159, 162, 165
Henry VIII, King, Commissioners of (see
    Royal Commissioners for the

Destruction of Shrines, the)
Herbert of Bosham, 84, 86–7
Holinshed, 90, 125–6, 128, 159
Holland, Miss Agnes (Mrs Bolton), 36–7,
    40–41, 49, 51–2, 90, 95, 104, 155
Holland, Rev F.J., Canon Residentiary of
    Canterbury, 36–7
Hope, W. St John, 67
Hory, Philip, 120
Hugh of Horsea (see Mauclerc, Hugh)
Hussee, John, 65
Hutton, W.H., 82

Icelandic Saga of Thomas, the, 25, 27
Il Pellegrino Inglese, 59, 130
Isabella, Queen (of England), 20

Jesuit Community, Farm Street, 52–3
Jesus College, Cambridge, 82
Joan of Navarre, Queen, 29, 141
John of Salisbury, 83–4, 87
John, King (of England), 20
Johnson, Dr Hewlett, 'Red Dean' of
    Canterbury, 95, 97–8, 100, 147

Kentish Gazette, the, x
King, Edward, Bishop of Lincoln, 44
King's School, Canterbury, 97, 147
Knight, Thomas, 120

Lady Margaret Chair of Divinity,
    Cambridge, 80
Lambeth Palace, 44, 56, 123, 130
Lambeth Palace Library, 123
Langton, Archbishop Stephen, xi, 23, 27, 46,
    144
Layton, Dr Richard, Archdeacon of
    Buckingham, 33, 110–12
Leach, Mr A.F., 67
Letter and Papers of Henry VIII, the, 118–19
Liddon, Dr H.P., 43
Life and Death of Sr Thomas More, the, 55, 63,
    122–4
*Life and Martyrdom of St Thomas Becket,
    Archbishop of Canterbury*, the, 53–4
Lincoln, 90, 92, 115, 117
Lincoln and Bennett, Messrs, 65
Lincoln's Inn, 97
Lindisfarne, 71
Linnean Society, the, 100–101
London, University of, 107
Louis VII, King of France, 1, 20, 25
Luttrell Psalter, the, 133

Malines Conversations, the, 80
'Man from Margate', the, 40, 49
Manchester, University of, 100
Manning, Cardinal Henry Edward, 53, 69
Marmion, poem by Sir Walter Scott, 71–2

Marquis of Barrow, the, 120
Martin, C. Trice, 67, 77
Martyrdom of Becket, site of, 8–9, 14, 25, 31
Mary Tudor, Queen, 50, 55, 68, 76, 92, 120, 122–3, 159
Mason, Canon A.J. (Arthur James), 37, 78, 80, 82–3, 86–7, 89–93, 99, 103–4, 123, 125, 128–30, 132–3, 136
Materials for the History of Thomas Becket, Archbishop of Canterbury, 83
Mauclerc, Hugh (Hugh of Horsea), 13, 48, 86, 89, 103
Milman, Henry Salusbury, 58–60, 63–5, 67, 77, 127–30, 132, 141, 143
Minutes of the Canterbury Chapter, the, 52, 97–9, 147–8
Mitchell, Rosslyn, Scottish MP, 79
Month, The, 53, 65
Montreuil, Madame de, 119, 126
Moore, Dr Edward, 68–9, 71–3, 75–7, 80, 82, 92, 97, 132–3, 165
More, St Thomas, 53, 55, 123–4
Morning Post, the, 48, 49
Morris, Fr John, 40, 52–8, 63, 65, 69, 77, 132, 138–9, 166
Morville, Hugh de, 4
Mottinstone, Lord, 98
Munich, University of, 157

Nilgen, Prof Ursula, 157
Noah, story of, 25
Norfolk, Duke of, 43
Nucius, Nycander, 122

Odet de Coligny, Cardinal Châtillon, ix–x, 135, 140–41, 147, 150
Official Account of the Reformation. Vindication of the Changes Recently Effected in England, 127
On Certain Human Remains Found in the Crypt of Canterbury Cathedral, 64
Oxford Dante, The, 69
Oxford Dante Society, the, 69
Oxford, University of, 69, 97, 123

Palmerston, Lord, 75
Pandulf, Papal Legate, 23
Parry, Dr, Bishop of Dover, 37
Parsons (or Persons), Fr Robert, 122
Pembroke College, Cambridge, 82
Pembroke College, Oxford, 69
Pennison, Sir William, 119
Petham, William, Prior of Christ Church, Canterbury, 144
Pole, Cardinal Reginald, 60, 90–91, 120, 122–3, 128, 141, 143
Polistorie, the, 20, 23, 27
Pollard, Richard, 115
Pollen, Fr J.H., 65, 125

Pontigny, 75, 77
Pope Leo XIII, 53
Pope Paul III, 90, 119, 122–3, 159, 162
Premonstratensian Abbey of Langdon, Kent, Abbot of, 111
Prescott, Peregrine, ix–x, 140
Priory of Christ Church, Canterbury, 14, 20, 46, 54, 66, 73, 84, 86, 89, 91, 111, 126, 131, 138, 149, 154, 165, 167
Privy Council, the, 59, 127–8, 130, 151
Proceedings of the Society of Antiquaries, the, 64
Pronk, Risto, ix–x
Pugh, William, Vesturer of Canterbury Cathedral, 66
Pusey, Edward, 43

Quadrilogus, the, 23, 25, 27
Queen Mary's Psalter, 32
Queen's College, Oxford, 69

Ravenna, 68–9, 73, 76, 165
Rawlinson, Miss Lisa, 36, 49, 51, 90
Reformation, English, ix, 32, 43, 58, 65
Reformation, the, 76, 90, 133, 136, 156
Régale of France, the, 20, 25
Relics and Shrines, 109, 144
Relics of St Thomas, The, 58
Restless Bones, 109
Revised Prayer Book, the (1927), 78–9, 82
Richard I, King, 20
Richard, Son of Einold of Bearstead, 16
Ro:Ba, 123–5, 131, 162
Robert of Cricklade, 25
Robertson, Canon W.A. Scott, 35, 52
Roger of Pont L'Evêque, Archbishop of York at time of Becket, 3, 6
Rolls Series, the, 66, 83
Roman Catholicism, Roman Catholic Church, 79, 82, 109
Rome, 43, 53, 79, 117, 119, 121, 127, 131, 157, 159, 162
Routledge, Canon Charles F., 35, 37, 49–53, 55, 60, 63–4, 69, 75, 77, 130, 132, 165
Royal Archaeological Institute, the, 52
Royal College of Surgeons, the, 37, 51, 55
Royal Commission on Ecclesiastical Discipline (1904–1906), 44, 78
Royal Commissioners for the Destruction of Shrines, the, ix, xi, 31, 33, 46, 52, 63, 65–6, 72–3, 75, 90, 92, 110, 114–17, 125, 131–3, 135, 143, 149–52, 154–5, 159, 161, 165–7
Royal Society of Arts, the, 97

St Alphege, 14, 136–7
St Augustine (of Canterbury), 156, 162
St Augustine's Abbey, Canterbury, 114, 125
St Bartholomew's Hospital, London, 95–6,

99–100, 160
St Candida, tomb of, 17, 19
St Chad, 73
St Cuthbert, 71–3, 76, 90, 116, 132, 157, 165
St Dunstan, 14
St Edmund Hall, Oxford, 69, 97, 100, 147
St Hugh of Lincoln, 90, 115
St John of Dalderby, 115
St Mary and St Nicholas, Corporation of, 148
St Odo, 137
St Osmond, tomb of, 17
St Paul's Cathedral, London, 43, 136
St Paul's Cross, 59, 127
St Peter's Collegiate School, Adelaide, 147
St Richard of Chichester, 90, 115, 128
St Swithin, 115–16, 129
St Wilfrid, 137
St William of York, 90, 117
Salisbury Cathedral, 44
Saltwood Castle, 4, 14
Sanders, Nicholas, 122
Sandwich, 3, 6
Santa Maria Maggiore, Basilica of (Rome), 157–8
Scott, Sir Walter, 71–2
Sheppard, Dr J. Brigstock, Seneschal of Canterbury, 35, 37, 49, 52, 77, 132, 139
Shirley, Canon John, 69, 95–100, 106–7, 109–10, 144, 147–9, 168–9
Siric, Archbishop of Canterbury, 137
Sixth Lambeth Conference (1920), 80
Smith, Dr Robert Payne, Dean of Canterbury, 37, 41–2
Society of Antiquaries, the, 58, 63–4, 67, 133, 141
Society of Jesus, The, 53
Somner, William, 144
Sox, David, 109, 144, 147
Standard, the, 58
Stanley, A.P. (Dean Stanley), 55, 117, 165
Stapleton, Thomas, 122, 124
Stour, River, xi, 3, 161
Stow, John, 27, 52, 58, 63, 65, 90, 125–6, 128, 159
Studies in Dante, 68–9
Studies in Dante, Textual Criticism of The Convivio and Miscellaneous Essays, 68–9
Sveinbjarnarson, Rajn, 20
Sykes, Very Rev Norman, Dean of Winchester ('NS'), 107, 109

Taylorian Institute, Oxford, 69
Theobald, Archbishop of Canterbury, 1
Thomas, William, Clerk to the Privy Council, 59–60, 130, 143, 153, 165–6
Thornden, Richard, Bishop of Dover, 46, 91–2, 154, 167

Thornton, W. Pugin, 35–8, 40–41, 48, 51–3, 55–6, 64–5, 77, 83, 90, 92, 96, 100–104, 132, 159
Times The, 35, 41–2, 49–53, 56, 58, 64, 97, 99–100, 109–10, 139, 147, 160
Tower of London, the, 114–15, 123, 128, 150, 161, 165
Tracy, William de, 4, 13, 84, 86
Trevor, Dr Jack, 95–6, 100, 107
Trinity College, Cambridge, 53
Trouble With Our Catholic Forefathers, The, 53
Truro Cathedral, 80

University College, London, 69
University of Kent, the, 100
Urry, Dr William, xi, 95–6, 100, 122, 132

Vallance, Mr Aymer, 40, 67, 77
Vanished Memorials of St Thomas of Canterbury, the, 58, 63
Venables, Very Rev Edmund, Precentor of Lincoln Cathedral, 52, 77, 132
Victoria, Queen, 43
Victoria History of the County of Durham, The, 71
Virgin Mary, the, 43

Walsingham, 157
Walter, Archbishop of Canterbury, 20
Walter of Colchester, 25
Walter, Prior of Canterbury, 23
Wells Theological College, 147
Westminster Abbey, 92, 98, 157
Whitchurch Canonicorum, Dorset, 17, 19
Wilckens, Prof Leonie von, 157
William, King of Scotland, 20
William of Canterbury, 82–3, 87
William of Sens, 17
William the Englishman, 17–19, 136
William I, King, 71
Winchester Cathedral, 44, 115–17, 129
Wiseman, Cardinal Nicholas, 53
Wolsey, Cardinal Thomas, 110
Wood, J.G., 67
Woodruff, Rev C. Eveleigh, Librarian to Dean and Chapter of Canterbury, 67–8, 77
Wootton, Nicholas, first Dean of Canterbury, 29, 141
Wordsworth, Christopher, 123–4
Wriothesley, Charles, 52, 58, 63, 65, 90, 125–6, 128, 159
Wriothesley, Thomas (First Earl of Southampton), 115–16, 120, 125
Wulfhelm, Archbishop of Canterbury, 137
Wyatt, Sir Thomas, 120–21

York, 90, 117
York Minster, 117